Resurrection

Resurrection

Interpreting the Easter Gospel

ROWAN WILLIAMS

The Pilgrim Press
New York

First published in Great Britain in 1982
by Darton, Longman & Todd Ltd

Library of Congress Cataloging in Publication Data

Williams, Rowan, 1950-
Resurrection: interpreting the Easter gospel.

Includes bibliographies and index.
1. Jesus Christ—Resurrection—Addresses, essays,
lectures.   I. Title.
BT481.W55   1984   232.9′7   84-16514
ISBN 0-8298-0727-6 (pbk.)

The Pilgrim Press, 132 West 31 Street, New York, NY 10001

Contents

Foreword by Paul S. Minear   vii

Preface   xi

Acknowledgements   xiii

Introduction   1

Chapter 1 The Judgement of Judgement:
Easter in Jerusalem   7

Chapter 2 Memory and Hope:
Easter in Galilee   29

Chapter 3 Communities of Resurrection   52

Chapter 4 Talking to a Stranger   76

Chapter 5 The Risen Body   100

Index   125

Foreword

I am happy to commend this book to an American audience because it stimulates fruitful thinking on an important topic. As Rowan Williams insists, all Christian doctrine is directly or indirectly a "reflection on Easter" (p. 3); accordingly he is quite right to call his work "an essay in irregular dogmatics." I think it is all the more rewarding for being irregular.

The publication of any British book in the United States brings to mind the old adage about two nations divided by the same language. This adage can be said to apply equally to divisions within America and within the church. And on no subject are these divisions more acute than on the character of resurrection. A theologian or an exegete may use precisely the same words as a colleague, but what he or she says may prevent mutual understanding rather than producing it.

Some time ago I was engaged in a colloquy with teachers and students in a prominent theological school. During the conversation I used the phrase "the presence of the risen Jesus." At that point the discussion was aborted. Almost in midsentence I was halted by the most influential theologian in the group, who asserted that such a phrase is either meaningless or misleading. Either it has no intelligible referent or it expresses an illusion that encourages self-deception on the part of pious Christians who rely on it. At first I was annoyed by this interruption and I wondered how best to respond. Since then I have come to appreciate the aptness of the protest. It is all too true that much speech about resurrection is quite devoid of meaning; it is also true that much speech consists of clichés which conceal self-centered and therefore idolatrous forms of faith. Of these dangers, Rowan Williams is keenly aware; they are implicit in the character of the term resurrection as "an ultimate metaphor."

Because this ultimate metaphor can be so opaque, the author frequently shifts the focus of attention to the metaphor of presence. He wants his readers to think through what it means to say that "Jesus is alive with God and also present to his followers." In making *presence* a key category, Williams joins Samuel Terrien in his choice of this as the central motif in biblical theology. In ultimate terms "God is the 'presence' to which all reality is present" (p. 29). Jesus is present to God in such a way that to believe in the resurrection is to believe that "God's presence is Jesus' presence" (p. 35). By making God present to his followers, Jesus defines their new identity. They become present to God, to Jesus, to themselves, to their fellow-believers, to their victims (p. 61). In a similar way, the presence of Jesus defines the identity of the community, an identity that is articulated in many ways, but especially in baptism and the eucharist (p. 63). But such a presence leaves Calvary a greater problem than ever, because Jesus always comes "as a stranger." His coming is "the return of the crucified to his crucifiers" (p. 37), a situation which both forces a new speech upon Jesus' enemies and at the same time reduces them to silence. His presence inculcates a deep suspicion of the efficacy of all language and it obliges witnesses to stand on "the frontier of any possible language" (p. 97). And since our language gives shape to our world, this new speech about death and life transforms the shape of our world.

It is probably significant that this book is entitled *Resurrection* and not "*The* Resurrection." This enables the author in each chapter to explore the multiple, unsuspected forms of resurrection in contemporary experience. Such exploration is slow-paced and therefore a slow pace is required in the reading. The reader finds much to ponder, much that leads the mind away from the page into the depths of memory. Introspection often arises from the fact that the author treats his readers not as credulous folk who want to believe in resurrection or as innocent victims of the world's brutalities, but as people who "have blood on their hands," as victimizers to whom their victims become present in judgment and grace, through the presence of Jesus as victim.

By the end of each chapter, Williams' thought has shifted from modern analogies to *the* resurrection of Jesus and to the New Testament accounts of that mystery. He leaves to biblical specialists the detailed exposition of those accounts, yet his imaginative approach helps us to make more sense of those texts. His insight into various details in the "apparition stories" is often uncanny. He is convinced that only through our own contemporary experience does the mystery of Good Friday and Easter become present to us (p. 59). When this happens, the "ultimate metaphor" again becomes real to us, furthering our penetration into the stories in the Gospels.

It is my hope that other American readers will welcome, as I do, this perceptive commentary on both resurrection and the biblical witnesses to *the* resurrection. Doubters will find here a target quite different from the conventional doctrines that have engendered their earlier skepticism. They may well sense their kinship with an author who suggests that any plausible reconstruction of the original appearances of Jesus is, "for that very reason, a dubious one" (p. 116). Believers will find not only new grounds for their faith but also a shocking challenge to their tendency to use that faith to enhance their own consolation and security. No bland and comfortable truth this, but the astringent discovery that resurrection has to do with all human violence in all human beings (pp. 54f.). Exegetes should welcome an author who not only talks about fresh ways of reading the ancient stories but also exemplifies those ways. By being subjectively involved in the thrust of the stories, Williams achieves a high degree of objectivity about them. The book should also encourage theologians who are searching for a language more consonant with the truth of the Gospel, a language that makes intelligible to earth-bound mortals the mysteries of a divine presence. And what about the clergy, for whom the book is primarily designed? Each week ministers celebrate the Easter message by invoking the presence of the risen Lord. That invocation initiates a period of worship in which the identity of the congregation is renewed as it becomes present again to God. A sensitive reading of *Resurrection* should alert ministers to the possible response by the Lord to that invocation; the prayer "Come, Lord" opens up a potentially infinite network of relations" (p. 60). In short, this book will provide profitable grist for any reader capable of thinking deeply on its subject.

Over the years, Cambridge University has produced many books on this theme, most noteworthy, perhaps, the books of B. F. Westcott, which appeared more than a century ago but which still merit inclusion on my shelves. This new study belongs within that succession. Thank you, Rowan Williams.

PAUL S. MINEAR

Preface

The episcopal district of Stepney has for some years had the excellent institution of an annual series of Lent Lectures for the clergy and church workers of the area, delivered at the Royal Foundation of St Katherine. When Bishop Jim Thompson generously invited me to lecture in 1981, I was sobered by the thought of trying to articulate a theology that would not be completely irrelevant to a divided, complex and deprived community, coming as I did from the relatively secure suburbs of Cambridge. But I was encouraged by the knowledge that this was also a vigorous and creative community, with vigorous and creative clergy whose response and criticism would be uniquely valuable. In other words, I hoped to learn at least as much as teach in this experience.

Nor was I disappointed. From week to week the reactions, sympathetic and questioning, constantly reshaped my own ideas and helped to make the course something of a co-operative venture. This book is not so much an edited transcript of the lectures given as the fruit of discussions and explorations initiated by those lectures. For all this I am abidingly grateful to those who listened and responded.

An extra dimension was added with the work of the International Anglican Doctrinal Commission at its first meeting in July 1981. Our debates about 'Church and Kingdom' prompted me to some fresh reflections, which have finally found their way into these pages. Many of my colleagues on the commission will, if they read this book, recognize themes and insights opened up by them at our sessions. My warmest thanks to them, and my apologies for any distortions and misunderstandings.

John Todd and Lesley Riddle at DLT have been—as ever—unfailingly sympathetic, patient and supportive. Jill Williamson spared valuable time from the care of a five-month-old daughter to produce an immaculate typescript; my gratitude to both of them. The late Fr Geoffrey Curtis, CR, deserves special mention: he was kind enough not only to attend the lectures, but also to set down his comments on paper, in a long letter which I received two days before he died. His remarks in this letter on baptism as the most fundamental Christian symbol, because of its speaking unequivocally of Christ's Easter *victory*, have a peculiar preciousness. And, above all, my wife Jane will know, I hope, how much of this book is the fruit of what she has shared with me of the Easter Gospel and the Christian hope.

Rowan Williams

Acknowledgements

The author and Chatto & Windus Ltd., for permission to reproduce the extract from *The Red & the Green* by Iris Murdoch on p. 76.

The University of Wales Press for permission to reproduce part of 'Mary Magdalene' by Saunders Lewis (translated by Gwyn Thomas) on p. 45, from *Presenting Saunders Lewis*, ed. Alun R. Jones & Gwyn Thomas.

The Scripture quotations in this publication are from the Revised Standard Version of the Bible copyrighted 1971 and 1952 by the Division of Christian Education of the National Council of the Churches of Christ in the USA.

Introduction

It has turned out to be more and more difficult to give an account of what sort of book this is meant to be; but writers ought to make some effort to state what it is they are aiming at, and what sort of methods are being employed. So let me attempt to clarify what I am up to. To begin with, this is not a work of 'scientific' New Testament exegesis: my main concern is not with sorting out the history and bias of the texts before us. However, it would be dishonest to ignore this dimension entirely, and I have at many points made certain assumptions about the texts and their provenance and concerns, based upon the scholarly work of the last few decades.[1] I have tried in the notes to give a little documentation in those cases where I have touched on particularly complex and debated matters, but have not on the whole undertaken to discuss these issues directly in the text.

What I *have* tried to discuss is how, as narratives, these Easter texts present us with a variety of 'significant patterns', imaginative approaches to the question of what it meant and means to say that Jesus who was deserted and executed is alive with God and also present to his followers. Thus I have looked at how, for Luke, a dramatic focus on Jerusalem is vital: Jesus is preached as 'risen' to those who actually, literally, condemned him to death. This is his 'significant pattern', perhaps the most obvious one in all the Gospels because he has gone on to tell a story of the beginnings of Christian

1

proclamation. Then there are the various stories of personal encounter with the risen Jesus, the stories of Paul, Peter, Magdalene, each one with its distinctive nuances: the resurrection must be shown to be good news to Paul as a persecutor, Peter as a betrayer, Mary simply as a lost and grieving human being. There is the question of the nature of these encounters: what is being said in the emphasis in so many passages on the initial 'strangeness' of the risen Lord? And there is the context of encounter, the significance of the tangible shared experience of a meal.

These are what I mean by 'significant patterns'. Taken overall, the resurrection stories, as stories, seem to be exploring various aspects of how the risen-ness of Jesus has to do with the sense of absolution by God, how the resurrection creates forgiven persons, whose relation with God and, derivatively, with each other, is transformed. They are stories that belong in a community which identifies and understands itself as forgiven, and traces its establishment as that sort of a community to the Easter event. I have written 'a community'; and of course I shall rightly be reminded that, when we are considering the origins of the New Testament, we are faced with a bewilderingly large number of sharply diverse— and sometimes mutually suspicious or hostile—communities. Yet although this is perfectly true, I am still obstinately persuaded that, in this area of belief in the resurrection, the patterns of interpretation do overlap; that belief in the risen-ness of Jesus (as reflected in the literary deposits of these communities) did not mean *radically* different things to different Christian groups. We are dealing with a family of beliefs, not a chaotic plurality. It may well be (and again the New Testament suggests as much) that there were groups for whom the cluster of 'paschal' events was not consciously explored or elaborated very much, and others, especially those in Paul's orbit, for whom these events were the subject of constant and searching reflection, even speculation. But this does not, I think, alter the fact that, where questions *were* raised about the meaning of Easter as the root of the 'meaning' of the existing community, the answers provided do have a certain homogeneity. They appear as aspects of a single process, a single and continuing discussion.

This is part of what this book aims to show. And if this is a correct perspective, it is not nonsense to speak of 'the' Church in the New Testament period: concern with its origins in Easter provides a unifying factor. Pressing this a little further: concern with its understanding of God as gracious, as restoring and remaking covenant, in connection with Easter, provides a unifying factor. And, building on this foundation, the chapters that follow attempt to see how our *present* understanding of God's graciousness in our shared life depends on the paschal story; how the New Testament narration of Calvary and Easter opens up on to the continuing process of re-assimilation and reflection in the Church's thinking and life.

So these chapters will involve a re-examination of certain central Christian doctrines, an effort to relate them afresh to the generative event at the source of the Church's life; but, while I hope they will suggest a way of seeing all doctrine as, essentially, reflection on Easter, I have not set out to develop an exposition of the whole intellectual structure of Christian dogmatics. And the discussion brings in, *en route*, a good deal of material on social and personal ethics, and even on 'ascetical theology', which doesn't quite fit within the conventional frontiers of systematic theology. Once again, though, I have felt the obligation to acknowledge my debts to a variety of recent writers in the field of doctrine (especially Ernst, Lossky, Metz, Moore and Schillebeeckx), and to relate what I have written to their more nuanced and professional discussions.

Nor do I particularly wish to define this book in terms of 'spiritual' or 'devotional' reading. I urgently and deeply want it to enhance Christian vision and animate Christian love, whatever its failings; and, if this is what a book of 'spirituality' is for, then I am happy to allow the definition. But I also want to resist the pressure to cordon off this area from critical theological (and historical) thinking. If the style of these chapters oscillates rather between the analytic and the impressionistic, that is the result of attempting to keep the devotional and the critical together in one interpretative process: the attempt may not be an unqualified success, but I still believe that it is worth trying to build some bridges here.

Perhaps the best thing I can do is to borrow Barth's phrase,[2] and call this an essay in 'irregular dogmatics'—'free discussion of the problems that arise for Church proclamation from the standpoint of the question of dogma'. Even this would be misleading if it suggested the acceptance of an agreed style of 'regular' or 'formal' dogmatics; Barth's distinction is not an easy one to maintain these days, chiefly because of the violent disagreements which persist about both the limits and the starting-point of a 'regular' dogmatics. However, Barth means his expression to stand for a theological style rather closer than some others to the actual preaching of the gospel: the commentary and the sermon (and perhaps the hymn?) are cases of 'irregular dogmatics'. What follows is neither commentary nor sermon, and it *does* set out to present a sustained theological argument. But it is admittedly done with more than half an eye to preaching (in the widest sense): the addresses from which this book first grew were by their nature somewhere between lectures, sermons and retreat conferences, and these pages will no doubt reflect such a mixture. If 'irregular dogmatics' is theology operating in that particular borderland, the term may well describe this work.

But this sort of theology is not absolved from the need for care and rigour. Barth lays down certain conditions for 'scientific' dogmatics, whether 'regular' or not:[3] it must be *direct* reflection on Church proclamation, *critical* reflection on Church proclamation, and reflection conducted with reference to what Scripture witnesses to, in an 'indemonstrable and unassuming attention to the sign of Holy Scripture around which the Church gathers and continually becomes the Church'.[4] In that sense, this work aims to be 'scientific', although I should want to broaden Barth's concern so as to include with 'proclamation' the historical corporate life, the shared activity, of the Church. The third chapter of this book is central in more than a merely sequential way: the attempt to criticize and test the Church's practice by reference to its professed allegiance to Jesus crucified and risen is near the heart of any serious theology. And in this at least we can heartily concur with Barth, that the Church is *never* the object of its own faith: it is necessarily under the judgement of what it points to. So, of course, is its theology.

This is one reason for the concern in the book's concluding chapters for the 'objective' pole of resurrection encounter. Jesus is not raised by our faith, but by God's prior act. Of course this is anything but straightforward to spell out at such an enormous historical distance; of course faith is not simply generated out of debatable historical assertions. Exactly what 'God's prior act' can mean is as unclear as it always is. Yet, as with the whole of Jesus' life, we are driven to speak of events which, without any unambiguous supernatural 'component' (the empty tomb itself remains a disputable sign), produce a kind of seismic shift in human speech and self-understanding—events which are creative in such a way that our talking about them is always exploratory and never exhaustive. This is the least that needs to be said about Easter: it is not to be reduced to a process of hard and inventive interpretative work by the disciples. What we have before us is far too confused and tentative for that; it points back into an obscurity rich and resourceful enough to be called nothing less than 'God acting'.

So the ultimate aim of the book is to point in that same direction, by discussing some of the ways in which 'resurrection communities', then and now, discover a gracious God in the return of Jesus to his disciples. And because such a return, of the betrayed and rejected one now clothed with power, is not self-evidently a sign of hope to the guilty, we must begin by looking closely at what the resurrection does to the idea of judgement itself: this is one obvious place where we may start to grasp why the resurrection is always gospel and never threat. We begin, then, in Jerusalem, with Luke's elaborate and skilful reconstruction of the origins of that Christian preaching which we still seek to serve and to vivify.

Notes

1. For instance, I have tacitly assumed not only that the Fourth Evangelist knew the traditions represented in the other gospels, especially Luke, but that he expected his audience to know something of them as well. I have taken it for granted that John 21 deliberately alludes to familiar stories of the call of the first apostles; and that, when Mary Magdalene appears in John 20, the evangelist expects us to recognize the name. And so on.
2. Karl Barth, *Church Dogmatics*, vol. 2, *The Doctrine of the Word of God*, part 1, tr. G. W. Bromiley (Edinburgh, T. and T. Clark, 1975), p. 277.
3. Ibid., pp. 280–4.
4. Ibid., p. 283.

CHAPTER ONE

The Judgement of Judgement: Easter in Jerusalem

1

The opening chapters of the Acts of the Apostles offer us a sharply-defined picture of the earliest preaching of the resurrection of Jesus. Although allowance has always to be made for the incorrigibly tidy mind of Luke, it is hard to deny that his reconstruction must bear some relation to the realities of that first preaching, if only because the resurrection was indeed first proclaimed in *Israel*; that is, it was first proclaimed to a specific audience with a particular history and memory, both of remote and of recent events and transactions. For that preaching must have presupposed (as Luke insists) the memory of the crucified: '*this* Jesus', the identifiable figure whose death was a public event, and whose sentence, however odd or irregular, belonged to a particular and observable bit of political process. But Luke goes further: this is not only an audience which knows about Jesus, an audience that has been a spectator of *ta peri Iesou tou Nazarenou*, 'the things concerning Jesus the Nazarene' (Luke 24:19). It is not a neutral audience, and it is not an innocent audience. In this event of the preaching of Jesus risen, there are no 'uninvolved bystanders'. For Luke, the apostles speak to an audience of participants, an audience with blood on its hands. The proclaiming of Jesus crucified and risen is not a matter of giving information; the

7

rhetoric of this preaching assumes that the hearers already belong in the story, that they are *agents*, that 'the things concerning Jesus' have concerned and will concern them.

This can—and must—be said without simply accepting at face-value Luke's general picture (shared with the other evangelists) of the Jewish people as such being guilty agents. The point is a structural one: the people of Jerusalem, and 'in' them 'all the house of Israel', and acting for them the rulers and elders—these are the ones whom the narrative identifies as the judges and killers of Jesus. Indeed, in Acts 4:27, Luke broadens his perspective to include, in an apocalyptic sweep, Jews and Gentiles alike, the 'kings of the earth', personified by Herod and Pilate, as well as the house of Israel; but they are still gathered 'in this city'. In Jerusalem, the judges assemble. Jew and Roman, priest and people, king and commoner: it is the 'city' thus constituted that condemns and rejects God's holy child; and it is in and to that city that the crucified is now proclaimed as risen. To accept this as the pattern of Luke's theological story-telling is not to entertain for a moment the appalling nonsense of a theory of generic Jewish guilt; though we shall see later in this chapter how lethally easy the transition from one to the other has often appeared. So far from arguing a generic guilt of any kind, Luke makes it clear that he is defining his audience, his 'Jerusalem', as the judges and condemners of Jesus: their guilt is historical, concrete and specific.

And this emerges most clearly, of course, when Luke presents us with the disciples preaching the resurrection to those who are most precisely the judges of Jesus. Although (as in Acts 2 and 3) Peter can say to all the 'men of Judaea and all who dwell in Jerusalem' (2:14) that '*you* crucified and killed' Jesus by the agency of 'lawless Gentile men' (2:23), that '*you* denied' him (3:13, 14), nonetheless there is a specific responsibility attaching to the leaders of Israel. Luke 22:66 shows us 'the assembly of the elders of the people . . . both chief priests and scribes' taking the initiative in delivering up Jesus to death. Acts 4: 5–6 parallels this closely: as in Jesus' trial, the assembly gathers on the day after the arrest (in this case, the arrest of Peter and John), and consists of 'rulers and

elders and scribes. . . with Annas the high priest and Caiaphas . . . and all who were of the high-priestly family'; and it
gathers 'in Jerusalem'—a pointless detail, regarded as mere
information, but reinforcing yet again the 'resonance' of the
image of the city for Luke, as the place where sentence is
pronounced.[1] The apostles stand in the name of Jesus before
the court that condemned Jesus: to this court they must·in
turn pronounce the sentence of God, the sentence implied in
the fact that the crucified and condemned is raised by God
and vindicated. He returns as the judge of his judges.

The court and city that condemned Jesus is still engaged
in judging and condemning him as it confronts his church.
And insofar as it continues to judge and condemn, it continues
to invite the judgement of its victim, whom God has approved
and exalted. So, at the simplest level, we have to do with a
straightforward reversal of roles: the condemned and the court
change places, the victim becomes the judge. And this as it
stands would have been a readily intelligible theological
move. The idea that those who are now poor and despised
will at the last day be endowed with the authority to judge
those who judged them is familiar enough from Jewish apocalyptic literature, from Daniel to Qumran and later. But the
gospel of the resurrection goes on to a more profound and
startling reversal. The exaltation of the condemned Jesus is
presented by the disciples not as threat but as promise and
hope. The condemning court, the murderous 'city', is indeed
judged as resisting the saving will of God; but that does not
mean that the will of God ceases to be saving. The rulers and
the people are in rebellion; yet they act 'in ignorance' (Acts
3:17; cf. Luke 23:34), and God still waits to be graciously
present in 'times of refreshing' (Acts 3:19). And grace is
released when the judges *turn* to their victim and recognize
him as their hope and their saviour.

Healing occurs 'by the name of Jesus Christ of Nazareth'
(Acts 4:10): the apostles stand before the court on account of
an act of saving and restoration, and this miracle is a sign to
the judges that the saving power of God is to be recognized
and sought in the crucified—and nowhere else. 'There is no
other name under heaven given among men by which we

must be saved' (ibid. 4:12). It has been said by one of the greatest of British New Testament scholars and expositors that 'the kind of preaching represented by the Acts threw all its stress upon vindication rather than redemption';[2] and, in the sense that Luke has a very undeveloped theology of atonement or justification, this is unquestionably true. Yet redemption in the simplest sense of an offer of decisive and transforming hope is very much a part of this preaching. The promise of liberation is pervasively present in terms (to borrow again the words of the writer quoted above) of 'the rescue, by the vindicated one, of his own opponents'.[3] By his vindication, by God's judgement pronounced against human judgement, the crucified becomes himself a *vindicator*, a source of justification. And the sharp exclusivism of Acts 4:12 must be read strictly in this light: grace is released *only* in confrontation with the victim.

And if we turn from the preaching and witness of the disciples in these early chapters of Acts to the dramatic account of Saul's conversion in ch. 9, we find the same insight taken a stage further still. Saul is stopped on his journey by a vision of power and judgement: blinding light, an accusing voice. He responds—as might be expected—by addressing his accuser as 'Lord' (9:5), recognizing the hand of God in the event by which he is challenged and judged. And the reply identifies this 'Lord' as 'Jesus, whom you are persecuting'. The Lord names himself not only as Jesus, but as Jesus embodied in the particular present victims of Paul's violence: he *is* those whom Paul has oppressed, hurt, or killed. And yet the annihilating force of this judgement by the victim on the oppressor is in due course lifted by the same victim: Ananias comes to Saul, saying 'The Lord Jesus who appeared to you on the road by which you came, has sent me that you may regain your sight and be filled with the Holy Spirit' (9:17). The Lord who judges is the Lord who saves; the Lord who vindicates his oppressed witnesses also comes, in their words and hands, to save their oppressors—who are his as well. As with Peter and John before the priestly court, so once again the witnesses of Jesus proclaim the identity of the saving Lord with the crucified victim; and, in their own witness, offer themselves and their Lord as the one source of present hope for their judges. Luke has begun firmly in Jerusalem: the risen Jesus appears only in Jerusalem and its environs, and the disciples are enjoined to 'stay in the city' until the gift of the Spirit comes (Luke 24:49 and Acts 1:4). But 'beginning from Jerusalem' (ibid. 24:47, and cf. Acts 1:8), the witness gradually spreads. Wherever Jesus is to be found among his disciples and wherever he is oppressed and persecuted in his disciples becomes a 'Jerusalem', the city of rejection, the court of judgement. The stress on geographical continuity in the first chapters of Acts points up the fact that the resurrection is first preached to the guilty; once it is further established that the persecuted Church 'embodies' Jesus as victim, the definition of the oppressor, the identity of the condemning court, becomes ever wider. If Saul is persecuting believers in Damascus, there too is a 'Jerusalem', awaiting the good news of the resurrection. And Acts 9 represents the decisive turning-point in the universalizing of mission—it spreads not only to Samaria (as in 8) but to the Gentile world (Acts 9:15; 10, *passim*): it is a gospel for all.

2

What I have said so far suggests a provisional definition of the primary stage in preaching the resurrection as an invitation to *recognize one's victim as one's hope*. The crucified is God's chosen: it is with the victim, the condemned, that God identifies, and it is in the company of the victim, so to speak, that God is to be found, and nowhere else. And this is not simply to say, in the fashionable phrase, that God makes his own the cause of the poor and despised. We are not talking of 'the' poor and despised, 'the' victim in the abstract. The preaching of the resurrection, as we have seen, is not addressed to an abstract audience: the victim involved is the victim of the hearers. We are, insistently and relentlessly, in Jerusalem, confronted therefore with a victim who is *our* victim. When we make victims, when we embark on condemnation, exclusion, violence, the diminution or oppression of anyone, when we set ourselves up as judges, we are exposed to judgement (as Jesus himself asserts in Matt. 7:1–2), and we turn away from salvation. To hear the good news of salvation, to be converted, is to turn back to the condemned and rejected, acknowledging that there is hope nowhere else. One of the tragic paradoxes of Christian history (and far too often of present Christian actuality) is the employment of Acts 4:12 as the justification of a fierce Christian exclusivism. It is perennially tempting to make this (once again) an 'abstract' statement: only in Jesus is there salvation. But, as we have seen, the Jesus who is here preached as sole source of salvation is the particular victim of that court. If any insight may be generalized out of this saying, it is that salvation does not bypass the history and memory of guilt, but rather builds upon and from it. It is a distortion to read it away from this context, as a legitimation of oppressive and condemnatory strategies towards the unbeliever.

To judge is to be exposed to judgement. Conversion is the realization that this equation shows us where we look for our vindication: the relationship we have set up, of judge to victim, is first of all to be reversed and then transcended. When I have seen that judging exposes me to judgement, I see that my oppressive and condemnatory role in fact wounds and diminishes *me*, makes me liable before the court (again we may compare Jesus' words in Matt. 5:21–2). I am my own victim, no less than the one I judge, and that is why I need salvation, rescue from the trap of the judge–victim relationship, the gift of a relationship which is not of this kind. But this means that the judge–victim relationship must itself be transformed: I am not saved by forgetting or cancelling my memory of concrete guilt, the oppressive relations in which I am in fact inextricably involved. And so I must look to my partner: to the victim who alone can be the source of renewal and transformation.

The problem is that in ordinary human relationships, boundaries are very fluid indeed. Even in a single relationship, I may be *both* oppressor and victim (consider the immense manipulative power exerted by the 'longsuffering' mother of a large family in certain circumstances: genuinely exploited and victimized herself, she is capable of doing great psychological damage in return),[4] and I can also be involved in all manner of subtle collusions with both my oppressors and my victims. The human world is not one of clearly distinguishable bodies of oppressors and victims, those who inflict damage and those who bear it. Where is a 'pure' victim to be found? Part of the fascination of images of childhood has to do with the vision of innocence: the child, it seems, and the child alone, can be purely victim (this is the burden of Ivan's harrowing monologue on 'Rebellion' in *The Brothers Karamazov*).[5] Yet, without diminishing the weight of this insight, it is no less true to say that the 'innocence' of the child is largely to do with the child's unformed capacity for responsible choice. Is it possible to imagine a person capable of choice, of choosing oppressive violence, who is in fact *only* victim and never oppressor? If so, such would be the one victim whose judgement might be more than a reversal of roles: such a person could never merely assume the place of the condemner over against myself as the new victim. And so there would be the possibility of a *transformed* rather than an inverted relationship.

The 'pure victim' alone can be the merciful, the vindicating judge. What Christian preaching asserts is that conversion, return to the victim in hope, is possible because Jesus embodies the condition of a pure victim. Judgement here is also mercy and hope because of the quality of this particular victim. The New Testament writers often show a great interest in Jesus' attitude at his trial: there is no sense in which Jesus uses counter-violence of a verbal or any other variety. 'When he suffered, he did not threaten' (1 Pet. 2:23). And this fairly naive point is elaborated in the Fourth Gospel into an extraordinarily sophisticated reconstruction of the whole concept of 'judgement'. The tradition made it clear that Jesus offered no 'violence' to any who turned to him in hope: he accepts, he does not condemn, resist or exclude. His life is defined as embodying an unconditional and universal acceptance, untrammelled by social, ritual or racial exclusiveness (the woman, the Samaritan, the leper, the collaborator, the sexually delinquent, the Roman soldier, all receive grace and fellowship in Jesus). And the tradition also recorded Jesus' silent resignation at his trial. Out of this, John weaves his rich fabric: Jesus is indeed the world's judge because he is 'Son of man' (John 5:27), yet to be 'Son of man' is to be 'lifted up' in sacrifice (3:14: 12:23, 32–4) and to be the meat and drink offered for the life of the world (6:53). It has often been noted that John, who uses 'Son of man' as a title very sparingly, restricts its use almost entirely to contexts where sacrificial death is in question.[6] Jesus is judge because he is victim; and that very fact means that he is a judge who will not condemn.

'God sent the Son into the world, not to condemn the world, but that the world might be saved through him' (3:17). The Father, as such, will not judge (5:22): judgement belongs to the Son, because it is the Son who is concretely involved in the processes of violence and condemnation. In other words, the divine judgement on the world is *not* delivered from a supernatural plane, but is enacted within the relations of human beings to each other. Judgement is inseparable from the event in which the light of loving acceptance shines in the human world and is shut out by that world (3:19). Yet Jesus can say, 'I judge no one' (8:15), and 'I did not come to judge the world but to save the world' (12:47). Judgement is not an activity in which Jesus engages: it is an event in which his 'word', his image, his history, 'acts' in the world to convict and transform (12:48). There is no will to exclude. Jesus will not 'cast out' any: 'and this is the will of him who sent me, that I should lose nothing of all that he has given me, but raise it up at the last day' (6:39). The judgement effected by the presence of Jesus is 'just', it is not an expression of human partiality, because Jesus' work is solely to embody and enact the Father's will (5:30); and that will is for the acceptance of the whole world.

So Jesus, as a man perfectly obedient to the Father, consistently refuses the role of oppressor: he does no violence, he utters no condemnation, he has no will to exclude or diminish. So John interprets the simpler themes of universal mercy and non-resistance. It is this which enables us to see emerging the image of the one who in any violent relationship can only be victim: the pure victim, the lamb who bears the sins of the world, who can only suffer 'violence', never inflict it; a man who is essentially and archetypally victim. And Simone Weil points to a kind of adumbration of this in classical Greek tragedy, in which 'Fate', the transmission of destructive force, can only be halted when its destructiveness is absorbed and not transmitted:

> What is called Fate in Greek tragedy has been very badly misunderstood. There is no such agency apart from this conception of the curse, which, once produced by a crime, is handed down by men from one to another and cannot be destroyed except by the suffering of a pure victim obedient to God.[7]

The exaltation of Jesus to be judge, to share the ultimate authority of God, is thus God's proclamation to all earthly judges, to the condemning court and the hostile city, that it is the pure victim alone who can 'carry' the divine love, the divine opposition to violence, oppression and exclusion. And so far from being passive, it is the pure victim alone who is capable of creative action, the transformation of the human world, the release from the pendulum swing of attack and revenge. The victim as 'pure' victim is more than victim: when God receives and approves the condemned Jesus and returns him to his judges through the preaching of the Church, he transcends the world of oppressor–oppressed relations to create a new humanity, capable of other kinds of relation—between human beings, and between humanity and the Father. There is more to human interrelation than the opposition of the one who possesses coercive force or authority to condemn and the one who suffers it.

Yet this does also imply something about God's attitude to any and every victim. If God's love is shown in the pure victim, it is shown (as we have seen) as opposition to violence: so it is impossible to conceive of the Christian God identified with the oppressor in any relationship of violence. The powerless sufferer, whether 'innocent' or 'guilty', is the one who belongs with God, simply in virtue of being a victim; so that the saving presence of God is always to be sought and found

with the victim. Conversion is always turning to my victim—
even in circumstances where it is important to me to believe
in the rightness of my cause. For we are not here dealing with
law and morality; there are other kinds of judgement-as-dis-
cernment, discrimination and responsibility, which would require a different treatment. What is at issue is simply the
transaction that leads to exclusion, to the severance of any
relation of reciprocity. It may be unconscious, it may be
deliberate and wilfully damaging, it may appear unavoidable;
but as soon as such a transaction has occurred, God is with
the powerless, the excluded. And our hope is that he is to be
found as we return to our victims seeking reconciliation, seeking to find in renewed encounter with them the merciful and
transforming judgement of Jesus, the 'absolute' victim.

Part of the point in stressing this is to guard against an
easy sentimentalizing of the victim. Some people need to
believe that penitence towards the victim is an admission of
the innate and impregnable *moral* superiority of the excluded
or dispossessed. This (curiously) reduces my violence to a
kind of mistake: had I but recognized the virtue of my victim,
I should have seen that I had no 'right' to act as I did. The
hard thing to accept (and to write of) is that it is not unjust
or misplaced violence that needs penitence (what, after all, is
the definition of just or rightly-directed violence?), but the
oppressive, excluding act *as such*. But the pressure is very
strong towards the easier view that someone must be 'in the
right': I feel guilt about my violence, so it can't be me;
therefore it must be my victim. It is a pressure reflecting a
very deep, but nonetheless ambivalent, longing for simple
moral orderliness, and it must be regarded with the utmost
suspicion.

To take a particularly painful example: it is quite often said
by white liberals or radicals that 'there is no such thing as
black racism'. Apart from the fact that this is demonstrably
untrue (even if 'black racism' is in considerable part conditioned by white racism), the statement carries overtones of
the idea that the victimized group is intrinsically incapable
of the kind of violence from which it is suffering. And this in
fact obscures the real atrocity of racial oppression: racism is

not evil because its victims are good, it is evil because its victims are *human*. They share a common humanity, complete with its failings as well as its beauties, with their oppressors. If I do not grasp this, I am not really open to the possibility of ordinary human relationship with the victimized group. I 'atone' for my primal sin of oppression by according a superior instead of an inferior place to my victims, placing a moral scourge in their hands to beat me as once I beat them; and this is a travesty of the process of human reconciliation and restoration: my imagination is still trapped in the illusion that the basic and ultimate form of human relation is that between the powerful and the powerless. Even if this is translated into terms of moral superiority and inferiority, the structure remains the same, a 'master–slave' relationship in which one partner is defined by the other.

Examples could be multiplied of this process. The astonishing genocidal violence directed against the native peoples of North and South America has again led to a sometimes sentimental reverence for 'pre-Columbian' culture. Comparably, nearer home, the commitment to a belief in the superiority of 'working-class' values and culture on the part of some of the English literary intelligentsia in this century points to the same pressure towards atonement by a reversal of the moral as well as the political power structure. Insofar as these phenomena are a celebration of the humanity of the oppressed, a willingness to *receive* from those we have imagined have nothing to give, they are one of the most hopeful signs in our divided civilization. Insofar as they refuse to take seriously the possible transcendence of the oppressive relationship, they are profoundly *un*hopeful.

God is not 'with' the victim in order to make *us* victims; so the preaching of the resurrection affirms. Yet we seek some firm ground for a 'justice' that will invert the existing order to create new victims out of old oppressors—or, worse still, new victims out of 'neutrals'. One of the greatest historical tragedies of this century has been the fate of the Palestinian Arabs. Europe's attempt to atone for a nightmare of incalculable violence against the Jewish people has produced a new race of victims in the Palestinians, and so set up a further chain of terrorist counter-violence as a result of the violence (a violence which is often made to seem intrinsic to the existence of the State of Israel, especially by the inflexibility of its military and political establishment in recent years) offered to the indigenous Arab populations. It is a distressingly sharp illustration of the deadly circularity of oppression; and we should make no mistake about its origins in European Christian anti-semitism.[8]

Yet any society that revenges itself on those who have offered it violence stands in the same rank. We are still intensely preoccupied in this country with whether prison sentences are adequately punitive—with whether our legal counter-violence is sufficiently powerful. Even if we allow that coercion and retribution are unavoidable aspects of the life of a complex, extended society, the fact remains that our justice is so organized as to make victims, to exclude and to diminish, and that we are concerned to see that this diminution and exclusion is of at least equal force with the violence a criminal has inflicted. How difficult is it for us to see the face of God as victim in a criminal in prison? At least it is easier to see it in that other class of persons chronically subject to social violence, the mentally ill, whom we continue to treat as enemies of society, as people guilty of threatening and upsetting our order. Christ as criminal, Christ as madman, Christ as alcoholic vagrant: all this and more is implied in the unconditional identification of God with the victim.

The Romanian novelist, Petru Dumitriu, has, in a haunting passage, pressed this theme perhaps as far as it can go:

> It used to be fashionable . . . to approve of young terrorists. Now that they have gone rather too far, it is fashionable to condemn them. But this evening I have just heard that one of the young Moluccans imprisoned in Holland for hijacking and murdering hostages, having inflicted definitive and incurable psychological traumas on chance victims who were absolutely innocent—that he has hanged himself in his cell. And anyone hanged in his cell is Jesus Christ on his cross. My God, my God, why have you forsaken us?[9]

The offence of being invited to see the face of Christ in the suicide of a terrorist (and, as I write, there are still hunger-strikers in the prisons of Northern Ireland) is enormous. Any firm moral ground beneath our feet appears to give way, and we cannot do without it. And yet to make this repellent invitation is not to deny that the face of Christ is also in the terrorist's victims (Dumitriu makes this plain), not to say that God treats human outrage as if it did not matter, *not* to say that we are wrong to give way to pain and fury at meaningless slaughter. It is to remind ourselves that the hopelessness and self-loathing, even the impotent anger of the jailed murderer, all that constitutes him or her a trapped and helpless victim, must speak to us, in however distorted an accent, of the Lamb of God. Our necessary justice does not repair the breach in the world created by a terrorist's massacre, it creates a fresh breach, which we are all too willing to see as unbridgeable, as final. But if God is the enemy of all human diminution, he is there too: he is there as the 'unfinishedness' of our relation to the criminal, as the muted question, the half-heard cry for some unimaginable qualitative leap into reconciliation. He is there guaranteeing that we shall not forget even the most loathed and despised of victims. He judges our justice: not condemning it or inverting it, but transcending. It is the secret that Paul learned, of a divine justice, righteousness, which acts only to restore—what Luther so strangely called the 'passive righteousness' of God,[10] the justice that will not act against us, that is incapable of aggression or condemnation: the righteousness that makes righteous.

3

To recognize my victim as my hope involves the prior recognition of the fact that I victimize, and of the identity of my victim. Once again, if we return to the preaching of the apostles in Acts, we see this as the first stage: the execution of Jesus, as a remembered public event, is presented to the hearers as their responsibility, not a neutral fact. The formulation, 'Repent and believe', stresses that God's forgiveness

cannot be abstract and general: the authentic word of forgiveness, newness and resurrection is audible when we
acknowledge ourselves as oppressors and 'return' to our victims in the sense of learning who and where they are. It is
the process in which memory becomes *my* memory, the memory of a self with a story of responsibility. And to remember
in this way is to have restored to me part of the self that I
have diminished. We have already touched on the idea that
the diminution of another is also the diminution of the self,
making the oppressor or aggressor liable before the court. It
diminishes the possible range of my human relations, in the
first instance; and the diminution is compounded if I fail to
recognize it for what it is. If my memory of an act of violence
is not a memory involving the penitent and responsible sense
of a shared diminution, of an act injuring myself and my
victim, then my present consciousness is a diminished one—
in the extreme case, a diseased one. Many have written of the
'neutralizing' of memory in men like Adolf Eichmann;[11] more
recently, we might point to the same phenomenon in William
Calley and the other perpetrators of the My Lai massacre.
War, of course, particularly modern war, specializes in tech-
niques for avoiding the owning of one's actions. Most extremely of all, when memory cannot be neutralized, criminal
pathology is familiar with the amnesia that can (genuinely,
it seems) blot out the recollection of a traumatically violent
crime. William Golding, in a well-known episode of his *Lord
of the Flies*, shows the genesis of such a 'neutralization' after
the orgiastic dance that has led up to the murder of Simon:

> 'And look, Ralph,' Piggy glanced round quickly, then
> leaned close—'don't let on we was in that dance. Not to
> Samneric.'
> 'But we were! All of us!'
> Piggy shook his head.
> 'Not us till last. They never noticed in the dark. Anyway
> you said I was only on the outside—'
> 'So was I,' muttered Ralph, 'I was on the outside too.'
> Piggy nodded eagerly.

'That's right. We was on the outside. We never done nothing, we never seen nothing.'

The episode concludes (for it has not been a very successful attempt at oblivion):

Memory of the dance that none of them had attended shook all four boys convulsively.
'We left early.'[12]

There is no healing of memory until the memory itself is exposed, and exposed as a wound, a loss. Yet this must equally happen without its reappearing as a threat. We shall see in more detail in the next chapter how this can be understood in the light of the resurrection, but it is enough for the present to note this as an indispensable aspect of the process of restoration which resurrection involves. The word of forgiveness is not audible for the one who has not 'turned' to his or her past; and the degree to which an unreal or neutralized memory has come to dominate is the degree to which forgiveness is difficult. Ulrich Simon, in his *Theology of Auschwitz*,[13] has some terrifying pages on the impossibility of forgiveness for the perpetrators of the holocaust because they are not 'there' to be forgiven, they are shadows spinning on the path to self-annihilation.

And yet God holds and keeps open in his life, his 'memory', even such people. It is possible to be your own victim, too, and the violence you do to yourself is no less real than that which others do. So the camp commandant who has diminished and isolated himself by his violence, and compounded the injury to himself by refusing to own the memory of it, has still unwittingly left his past in the hands of God. If forgiveness is ever to be realized for him, it is not only the face of his victim which must be 'returned' to him, but his own forgotten face: the face of himself as his own victim, scarred and ruined by what he has done. He must see Christ, the saving victim, the merciful judge, not only in the victim whose blood is on his hands but in the self he could and would not be, the self he has decided against:[14] in the first instance, the non-violent, the non-oppressive self he has rejected, then also in the penitent self he has refused to become in burying or neutralizing his memories.

There is no justification without the resurrection. Ivan Karamazov cries out against the prospect of an ultimate reconciliation between victim and murderer based on a recognition of God's justice, and he is right. But what if that justice is not the vindication of a divine plan, but the revelation of God's identity in the insulted and injured, the uncovering of all forgotten wounds, so as to open up again the possibility of fresh relation, growth into healing? God does not shoulder aside the victim to pronounce an empty and formal acquittal to the oppressor (what right has anyone to forgive on behalf of another? What right has any Gentile to 'forgive' those who organized the Holocaust? What right has a non-worldly, a discarnate, God to forgive any human being?):[15] he is not to be found, his grace and mercy are not to be found, anywhere but in the past of human violence. God as gracious 'occurs', is manifest, only in the resurrection of the crucified. 'There is salvation in no one else.' No amount of the rhetoric of 'self-transcendence' can substitute for the recovery of the self, the self as the memory of crucifixion and crucifying: there are no dead selves discarded or buried to be the foundation-stones of new identities, because God is the God who opens our graves and gives back the past.

Human beings are perennially vulnerable to the temptation of arrogating divinity to themselves. It is a temptation manifest in the refusal to accept finitude, creatureliness and dependence—what Ernest Becker has called the 'causa sui project',[16] the delusion that the world is my world, a world controllable by my will and judgement. But it is no less manifest in what we might call the apocalyptic delusion, the belief that we can stop, reverse or cancel history, that we can assume the 'divine' prerogative of acting with decisive finality in the affairs of the world, that we can 'make an end'. Because our human history is marked by an ultimate severing of relations in death,[17] and because death is something we can inflict (though not resist), it is not surprising that we nurture this delusion. It can be a source of relief: by the murder of another, by the obliteration of a race, by the consignment of someone to the isolation of prison or hospital, by the suffocation of my own memory, I can be free ('A little water clears us of this deed'). Or it can be a source of horror and despair: death ends all hope of reconciliation, it fixes in an everlasting rictus the hopeless grimace of failure in a relationship. We may stand appalled at our destructiveness, believing that we have indeed destroyed, annihilated, our possibilities.

The resurrection as symbol declares precisely our incapacity for apocalyptic destruction—and equally declares that the 'divine prerogative' of destruction is in any case a fantasy. God's act is faithful to his character as creator, and he will destroy no part of this world: his apocalyptic act is one of restoration, the opening of the book which contains all history. 'God' is that to which all things are present, so theology traditionally affirms: so, through the mediation of God, all things can be made present to *us* again, present through his presence. The concept of God's 'memory' as holding or keeping open the past overthrows the delusion that our violence is final and irremediable. But what takes us further than this and ensures that the 'memory' of God is a saving fact, neither a menacing nor a neutral one, is the conviction that God's presence to the world is neither menacing nor neutral. God identifies with the victims in the world's history: we learn this in the fact that the bearer of his grace and power in our history is one who can be described as 'purely' victim, in no way the perpetrator of diminishing and excluding violence. So that God's 'memory' is the victims' memory: yet because the life of God is not a life with worldly limits, worldly constraints on its possibilities, the memory of suffering here is— we might say—embedded in an inexhaustible life. God receives the victim's pain into an infinite selfhood and self-presence; and so when he returns to us the memory of what has been done, it is as a memory inseparably bound to a reality which guarantees the hope of healing because its resources and possibilities cannot be exhausted or extinguished by the world's destructiveness.

Thus the risen one judges not only our judgement but our fear of judgement. His condemnation is pronounced against the whole system of earthly condemnation, and the structures of mutual rejection and fear in which human beings live are challenged in the most direct way. In the light of the return to us of the crucified, we can learn to interpret our world as it has been in these terms of mutual rejection, to see our human history as one of condemnatory and excluding violence. We are all of us, in some measure, shut off from each other: our own individual options for violence fade into an overall background of endemic violence. We are born into a world where there is *already* a history of oppression and victimization: our moral and spiritual growth does not occur in a vacuum. And so, before we can be conscious of it, the system of oppressor–victim relations absorbs us. It is this 'already' which theology (sometimes rather unhelpfully) refers to as original sin—the sense of a primordial 'diminution' from which we all suffer before ever we are capable of understanding or choice. When we diminish or victimize ourselves in our violence to others, we are in part responding to the incomprehensible and buried memory of 'diminutions' experienced in the pre- or semi-conscious state of our earliest years—or months or days. Even in the most loving of parent–child relations, unconscious and unintended violence can occur; and it has taken a very long time for the realization to dawn that the experience of birth itself may be the primary and traumatic deprivation, 'robbery with violence'.

This is not to deny that we need to speak of moral responsibility, of conscious options for and against violence, of guilt; yet if the relations of human beings have in them an irreducible element of mutual diminution or deprivation, 'violent' displacement or exclusion, we can understand that fundamental and pervasive lack in the human world of a sense of being affirmed, accepted, given a place, given a share, which generates the impulse towards the self-protective, self-affirming exclusion and diminution of others. It has been said that Jesus was betrayed in the 'lost childhood of Judas'; Georges Bernanos could write boldly of Hitler as an *enfant humilié*,[18] responding with pathological intensity and on an enormous scale to a profound experience (in no way understood, faced or assimilated) of deprivation. But any act of violence, even the most muted or symbolically displaced, reflects such a response to primordial diminution.

In this sense, we are all victims, and the mythological instinct is a sound one which represents the human race as the collective victim of the devil, a personified principle of deprivation, the great 'despoiler'. Yet such a discovery can only be made—as I have tried to show in this chapter—by beginning from the particular facts of the violence for which I am responsible, not by a bland generalization. By discovering my past of oppression, I can discover my own self-diminution in the process; and in pressing back to the source of this vicious spiral, I discover the primary lack of wholeness, the primary deprivation, which is a part of belonging to the single human story.

But the freedom, the 'space', to undertake this process of discovery requires the presence of the 'pure victim', the symbolic figure who transcends the order of human violence, a figure first to be identified with my victim, then with myself, in a continuing process of mediation and reinterpretation (we shall be looking at this in more detail in the fourth chapter). And the gospel of the resurrection offers Jesus crucified as such a figure. There are obvious problems which traditional Christian theology has wrestled with valiantly and none too successfully for centuries. If Jesus belongs to the same human story as we do, does he not suffer the same 'primary deprivation'? Do we have to introduce the dogma of the immaculate conception of Mary in order to avoid seeing Jesus as an inheritor of endemic violence? Is his humanity 'fallen' or 'unfallen'? and so on. These are very far from being scholastic technicalities; yet we may fairly ask whether there is any answer to them that is free of some degree of paradox. Jesus is unquestionably within the human story, but he is remembered as one who absorbed and did not transmit deprivation and violence. And that is hopelessly paradoxical. What is more, we cannot resolve the problem by offering a 'psychobiography' of Jesus of Nazareth which would explain what he did with the human inheritance of violence in his own particular interior ecology. It is true (as New Testament scholars have been telling us for decades) that we cannot confidently reach back behind the preached Christ to a simple, neutral 'Jesus of history'. That piece of particular human memory has become—irrevocably, it seems—a symbol, at once a vehicle of human self-interpretation, and a challenge to human self-interpretation. Yet its effective force as a symbol still depends on its particular location, upon its being a point that can be plotted in the human story—upon Jesus being thus and not otherwise. We may not be able to gauge in neutral terms the accuracy of the remembered story of Jesus, but we can at least recognize that its particular contours were by no means insignificant to the first believers.[19]

So we return to our starting-point. The preaching of Jesus crucified and raised occurs in a specific human context in which Jesus and his death are available in the public memory. *This* man and his way of living and dying, this man rather than any other, is exalted, approved and vindicated. The preaching of the resurrection takes this out of the realm of mere report by its address to a particular audience, its requirement that they see themselves as guilty of the violence of the cross and turn back to their victim. And this can be done in hope precisely because it is *this* man and no other who is involved, the pure victim, the carrier of mercy and acceptance. Thus the process begins by which the particularity of Jesus crucified and proclaimed as Saviour in Jerusalem becomes a universal symbol, the focus and pivot of a fresh and transforming interpretation of all human reality. The solidity and resourcefulness of the symbol can be grounded only in this process of interpretation, not straightforwardly in historical research; although the historical ground remains a kind of limit condition for the symbol (if certain facts were to be demonstrated about the life and character of Jesus, that he was a violent and exploitative personality, for instance, the symbol would be reduced to being only a convenient fiction, and its force would be very different).

'There is therefore now no condemnation', wrote Paul, 'for those who are in Christ Jesus' (Rom. 8:1). Condemnation is condemned in him; those who come to be 'in' Jesus, who live in, or under, or by the resource and power of the symbol of cross and resurrection, have passed through God's ultimate judgement. As the author of the Fourth Gospel had grasped, the last day has already happened for them. This does not mean that they are no longer under judgement in the sense that their lives are subject to no norm or model. God's judgement operates in the gospel of the resurrection to bring men and women out of the slavery and deprivation of violence and mutual exclusion into a new creation, whose 'law' is Christ.[20] The community of those in Christ can thus be both a penitent and a hopeful community, a community, that is, capable of recovering its individual and corporate history in trust (we shall be exploring this further in the third chapter). And it is a community whose concern, in living under Christ's 'law', is to stand against oppression, exclusion and violence, to stand *for* the kind of human relation—and human–divine relation—which transcends the oppressor–oppressed bond.

The apostles preached the risen Christ to Jerusalem because they had themselves 'seen the Lord'. And if our understanding of resurrection as developed in this chapter is accurate, their seeing of the Lord must also have been a giving-back of the past of guilt and hurt. So in the next chapter we shall turn to an examination of some of the apparition stories in the Gospels, in the light of what has already been said about the restoration and healing of memory, and attempt to sort out further the connections already outlined between memory and liberation, memory and mission, memory and renewed responsibility. How is the resurrection of the past actually creative of a new and 'empowered' human identity? If in this chapter we have been discussing resurrection as the ground of justification, we need now to see how it is equally the ground of sanctification, the growth of the redeemed life in the spirit of each man and woman.

Notes

1. The point is made in, for example, G. W. H. Lampe's commentary on Acts in *Peake's Commentary on the Bible*, ed. Matthew Black and H. H. Rowley (Nelson 1962), p. 891, § 778 i (cf. p. 892, § 779f).

2. C. F. D. Moule, *The Phenomenon of the New Testament* (SCM 1967), pp. 96–7.
3. Ibid., p. 95.
4. For a classic instance, see Mary Barnes and Joseph Berke, *Mary Barnes. Two Accounts of a Journey through Madness* (McGibbon & Kee 1971, and Penguin Books 1973), on the role of Mary's mother; and cf. the remarks of Ida Görres in *Broken Lights. Diaries and Letters, 1951–1959* (Burns & Oates 1964), p. 269: 'I'm inclined to think that one root of the fascination of "the mystique of suffering" is the peculiar fashion in which it fuses charity . . . with the desire for power'.
5. Part II, Book 5, ch. 4.
6. See, for example, C. K. Barrett, *The Gospel According to St John* (SPCK 1965), p. 60.
7. Simone Weil, *Intimations of Christianity among the Ancient Greeks* (RKP 1957), p. 60.
8. On this whole question, see the deliberately partisan and provocative book of Lucas Grollenberg, *Palestine Comes First* (SCM 1980), p. 118 on anti-semitism as a European and Christian phenomenon, though this is not a theme which looms very large in the book, and could be more clearly stated.
9. *Au Dieu inconnu* (Seuil, Paris, 1979), p. 26.
10. See Gordon Rupp, *The Righteousness of God* (Hodder & Stoughton 1953), on this theme in Luther.
11. See especially the remarks of Thomas Merton in *Conjectures of a Guilty Bystander* (Burns & Oates 1968), pp. 261–5; and *Raids on the Unspeakable* (Burns & Oates 1977), pp. 29–33.
12. *Lord of the Flies* (Faber 1954), pp. 174–5.
13. (SPCK 1967), ch. 6.
14. This is the controlling theme of Sebastian Moore's *The Crucified is No Stranger* (DLT 1977).
15. That God has no 'right' to forgive *on behalf of* the rejected and injured is, of course, the ground of Ivan Karamazov's refusal of any ultimate harmonization of the moral world, in his monologue already referred to (n 5, above).
16. Ernest Becker, *The Denial of Death* (Macmillan, New York and London, 1973).
17. We shall return to this theme later on, in chapter 3 of this book.
18. See Robert Speaight, *Georges Bernanos. A Study of the Man and the Writer* (Collins & Harvill 1973), pp. 230–1.
19. Recent New Testament scholarship has become a great deal more persuaded of this; see, for example, Gustaf Aulén's survey, *Jesus in Contemporary Historical Research* (SPCK 1976).
20. The figure of Christ in the Pauline epistles more and more takes on the attributes formerly ascribed to the pre-existent Torah, the ideal Law in God's mind, the divine plan in creation; see, e.g., W. D. Davies, *Paul and Rabbinic Judaism* (2nd edn, SPCK 1955), ch. 7.

CHAPTER TWO

Memory and Hope: Easter in Galilee

1

God is the agency that gives us back our memories, because God is the 'presence' to which all reality is present. We have already begun to see how this returning of memory is very far from being a congenial and painless process, because memory is the memory of our responsibility for rejection and injury, for diminution of self and others. And yet the refusal or denial of memory is likewise diminution, perhaps the deepest diminution of all. If the whole self is the concern and the theatre of God's saving work, then the past of the self must be included in the scope of this work. And this is so because the self at any given moment is a *made* self: it is not a solid, independent machine for deciding and acting efficiently or rationally in response to stimuli, but is itself a process, fluid and elusive, whose present range of possible responses is part of a developing story. The self *is*—one might say—what the past is doing now, it is the process in which a particular set of 'given' events and processes and options crystallizes now in a new set of particular options, responses and determinations, providing a resource of given past-ness out of which the next decision and action can flow. It is continuity; and so it is necessarily memory—continuity seen as the shape of a unique story, *my* story, which I now own, acknowledge, as mine. To be a self is to own such a story: to

29

act as a self is to act out of the awareness of this resource of a particular past.

This may seem a bit laboured or abstruse. But we do need to be careful not to fall into the trap of regarding 'the self' (or the 'soul', or whatever) as a spring of action determined by pure will[1] or as a timeless substance operating by pure reason. Both these myths represent attempts to guarantee that the self remains transcendent of its surroundings, free and (possibly) immortal—that it is more than an 'automatic' system of conditioned reflexes. But it might be truer to say that the self's transcendence is in its memory, precisely in its recollection *now* of another reality, a past reality, both distinct from and part of the present situation. Memory affirms that the present situation has a context; it, like the self, is part of a continuity, it is 'made' and so it is not immutable. By learning that situations have wider contexts, we learn a measure of freedom or detachment from (or transcendence of) the limits of the present.[2] Things may be otherwise; change occurs.

This is as true at the corporate as at the individual level. Eliot wrote, in *Little Gidding*, that 'A people without history/ Is not redeemed from time'. This tantalizingly ambiguous phrase can be read as saying, 'To lose one's history is not the same as being liberated from the limitations of life in time', or, more strongly, 'To lose one's history is to be *condemned* to an "unredeemed" condition, to absolute bondage to the temporal process.' On either reading, to be 'redeemed from time', to be liberated from the sense of the present and the future as a trap and an enslavement, requires historical awareness. When we see societies losing or suppressing their past, we rightly conclude that they are unfree, diseased, or corrupt: either they are oppressed by an alien power intent on destroying their roots and identity (the classic case being the colonial contempt for indigenous memory and culture), or they are engaged in an internal repression, a conscious or unconscious restriction of present human possibilities (and in this connection, the rewriting of history in certain kinds of totalitarian states is in effect a *loss* of history). Hence the importance for all national 'liberation movements' of a recovery of the past:

think of the political weight and imaginative force of the name 'Zimbabwe', for instance.[3] The same is true of liberation movements of a different sort. We can point to the proliferation of feminist studies of women's role in history or literature as illustrating the same process of 'recovery'.

Johann-Baptist Metz, who has given more attention than most contemporary theologians to the problem of memory, has written of memory as 'the means by which reason [can] become practical as freedom',[4] and refers to Marcuse's linking of memory with imagination, both being a means for the *critical* understanding of the present, 'a way of mediation that can momentarily at least break through the omnipresent power of the given facts'.[5] When the power of given present facts is challenged as we come to see the present situation as the issue of contingent processes and choices, we gain resources for new decision, and openness to new stages of process. We learn to act and to hope. Memory, at this level, can be the ground of hope, and there is no authentic hope without memory.

This may help us to understand the way in which Augustine in his *Confessions* takes the bold step of identifying memory with 'spirit', especially as he embarks in Book X upon his great quest for God in the structure of human self-awareness. Memory is the 'self', because it is my presence to myself, the way in which I constitute myself and understand myself as a subject with a continuous history of experience.[6] I am not trapped and confined in the present moment: as a conscious subject with a remembered past, I 'transcend' these limitations. I can understand them, put them in perspective, move on from and through them. Thus whatever stimulates and nourishes 'transcendence' in this sense has to do with presence to myself, and so with memory. Without this, my bondage is complete. It is no accident that long-term prisoners—in concentration camps or labour camps, for instance—have so often felt the need to 'recover' not only their own past, but a whole cultural or religious tradition, a shared past which can genuinely be seen as an alternative and liberating reality.[7] To affirm one's identity, value, solidity, reality in situations where this is being systematically crushed, to affirm that one is 'spirit' (an unsatisfactory word, but the best we have), involves the owning, the recovering of a past, a liberating memory.

Yet here we come up against the problem touched upon in the first chapter. What if the past that is returned or recovered is a record of guilt, hurt and diminution? The memory I have to recover is that of my particular, unalterable past; and if that is a memory whose recollection is unbearably painful, the record of a moral and spiritual 'shrinkage' or deprivation, how is it liberating? What of the destructive power of 'the bitterness which in human life so often succeeds what at least in memory seems fraught with promise', the 'seeds of corruption' sown unseen?[8] Memory may show us how we have been 'trapped' at various points in the past, how what we supposed to be a decision transcending circumstances was in fact subtly determined by unnoticed or undervalued factors, and so condemned us to the vicious consequences of actions based upon illusion. For we can all testify to the hard truth that much of our memory is the recollection of vast self-deceptions.

> And last, the rending pain of re-enactment
> Of all that you have done, and been; the shame
> Of motives late revealed, and the awareness
> Of things ill done and done to others' harm
> Which once you took for exercise of virtue.
> (*Little Gidding*, II. 138–42)

Forgiveness, we have already insisted, is never abstract. It is addressed to precisely these particularities. If forgiveness is liberation, it is also a recovery of the past in hope, a return of memory, in which what is potentially threatening, destructive, despair-inducing, in the past is transfigured into the ground of hope, I wrote earlier of how the vision of the victim as saviour operates to remove threat and fear: it makes it possible for us to remember, because we are assured that our destructiveness is not the last word. How, then, does forgiveness work? How does the restoration of memory work not only to remove our fear but positively to turn the past of guilt and injury into a resource, the soil on which a richer identity may grow? There is a pious cliché to the effect that the saints in heaven rejoice over their sins because they have been the occasions of such great mercy (and we may recall too the 'happy fault', the 'necessary sin', of which the Easter Proclamation, the *Exsultet*, speaks). Our job in what follows is to explore how the gospel of the resurrection makes sense of such language.

2

We shall begin this investigation by turning to one of the resurrection narratives of the Fourth Gospel, a story which illustrates a curious and enigmatic theme found also in two of the Synoptic Gospels: 'He is going before you to Galilee' (Mark 16:7). In the first chapter we considered the importance of *Jerusalem* as the place where the risen Jesus is first preached; but the apparitions in Galilee form an equally significant part of the resurrection tradition in Matthew and (probably) Mark. Matthew, it has been suggested,[9] wants to move the centre of theological gravity decisively away from the heart of old Israel. Mark's reference to resurrection appearances, or the promise of them, in Galilee is notoriously far more puzzling. But it is John who takes up the Galilee tradition and weaves it into a strange and compelling Galilean 'fantasia'—strange not least because of its fragmentary nature, its isolation from the rest of the Gospel. Whether it is a deliberately added appendix or supplement, or a draft conclusion, originally discarded, and later clumsily edited and joined on by the evangelist's community, remains obscure. Yet it is a sophisticated and highly-charged narrative, consciously pulling together a great many threads, and it has a particular pertinence to our theme of recovering the past.

The disciples are shown as the chapter opens making a decision to 'return': they go to their nets, go back to their job. John never uses elsewhere the synoptic traditions of the apostles being called from their nets, but this story suggests pretty plainly that he was familiar with such traditions. He seems to be inviting us to think of the resurrection manifestation as coming to disciples who, after Calvary, are 'as if' returned to their earliest circumstances: it is as if Jesus had never been. Their recovery of him is as drastically new as was their first encounter. The stranger on the shore points them to where they may find abundance and sustinence: and in that moment the connection is made. 'It is the Lord.' The memory of Jesus returns, it is no longer as if he had never been. What he once gave, he still gives, life in abundance. And as he once broke bread with them, so he does now. He has food already, he does not *need* the fish the apostles have caught, yet he invites them to bring what they have to share with him, as he gives what he has to share with them. It is in this sharing that they perceive who the stranger is (though he is still, notice, a stranger: it would be *possible*, though superfluous, to ask him who he is). He has called them as he called them at first, and they recognize both him and themselves in that calling.

Yet the recognition must go deeper still. The disciples recognize Jesus as Lord and themselves as disciples; but that buried past in which they were his disciples, the past that is slowly returning, is also the past of their desertion and failure. After the meal, Jesus' threefold interrogation of Peter recapitulates Peter's threefold denial. As on his first appearance before Jesus in the Gospel (1:42), he is addressed as 'Simon, son of John'; but he is at the same moment being reminded that he is no longer simply 'Simon, son of John'. He is Peter the apostle; the failed apostle. Some have noted that the 'charcoal fire' (*anthrakia*) burning on the shore echoes the mention of the *anthrakia* burning in the High Priest's courtyard on another chilly morning (18:18), the fire at which Peter warms himself as he denies his Lord. If this is deliberate (and why not? John, or whoever finally edited this episode, does not waste time with merely picturesque details), it is a touch of almost Proustian subtlety. Simon has to recognize himself as betrayer: that is part of the past that makes him who he is. If he is to be called again, if he can again become a true apostle, the 'Peter' that he is in the purpose of Jesus rather than the Simon who runs back into the cosy obscurity of 'ordinary' life, his failure must be assimilated, lived through again and brought to good and not to destructive issue.

The recovery of memory is radically different from regression. Memory is never simply the recovery of lost innocence: Peter is *not* Simon, the apostles are *not* fishermen. If there is a going back, a 'return to Galilee', it is not to stay there. For Matthew (28:16ff), the eleven go to Galilee to be sent 'into all the world'; for John, Galilee is the place where the past is recovered in such a way as to make it the foundation for a new and extended identity, the soil on which a redeemed future may grow. If the apostles are to be sent *now*, it is as men who have encountered afresh the Lord who sends them; and he comes now to men whose history is one of initial hope and promise, followed by betrayal and emptiness. They are called now and sent now as forgiven men: their apostasy does not alter God's purpose. And so too their apostasy does not take away the identity that God's purpose gives them. Simon is still, in the eyes of God, Peter. What he has to learn is that his betrayal does not make God betray, so that his calling as Peter, as rock of the apostolic faith, is still there, waiting to be lived out.

On the far side of the resurrection, vocation and forgiveness occur together, always and inseparably. Simply to be given back the past of wrong and hurt is not of itself a transaction of grace: we have already seen how the bare, context-less recovery of memory can be something regarded only with terror and despair. What happens in the resurrection is that this memory is given back in a particular kind of context—in the presence of Jesus. I wrote at the beginning of this chapter that 'God is the "presence" to which all reality is present'. So to be with God is to be (potentially) present to, aware of, all of one's self and one's past; which is why, as St John repeatedly reminds us, presence to God can be excruciating, and some will hate and reject the possibility. But when that God is revealed and embodied and 'specified' in Jesus, the victim who will not condemn, we can receive it. If God's presence is Jesus' presence, the past can be borne. For the Lord who returns, bringing our memory with him, is, as he always was, the Lord who waits on our love: 'Simon, son of John, do you love me?' He asks us to respond to him, to engage with him; he proposes a new stage of relationship.

Peter's fellowship with the Lord is not over, not ruined, it still exists and is alive because Jesus invites him to explore it further. Here the past is returned within a lived relationship that is evidently moving and growing. To know that Jesus still invites is to know that he accepts, forgives, bears and absorbs the hurt done: to hear the invitation is to know oneself forgiven, and *vice versa*.

Thus the memory of failure is in this context the indispensable basis of a calling forward in hope. Peter, in being present to Jesus, becomes—painfully and nakedly—present to himself: but that restoration to him of an identity of failure is also the restoration of an identity of hope. The presence of Jesus, still faithful, still calling, inviting his followers to love him, opens out the past in grace. And what Peter may learn is that wherever he may find himself, however he may fall, his life is constantly capable of being opened to God's creative grace: God's presence in Jesus will not fail him. The inconstant, vulnerable decisions and commitments of human beings, endlessly liable to destructive illusion, are set against the backcloth of God's constant decision and eternal commitment, his everlasting invitation to and 'making space' for his creatures. And it is this kind of juxtaposition that led the New Testament writers to see Jesus as himself 'eternally' embodying that commitment and call—for John, the eternal Word, for Paul (or his disciple and continuator in the later epistles), the pre-existent 'Head of Creation', the divine Wisdom, for Matthew, more simply, the one who has promised to be with the Church 'to the end of the age' (28:20), the 'faithful witness' of the Apocalypse (Rev: 1.5).

To be present to myself before the risen Jesus is to be present to God, and to know that the presence signifies mercy, acceptance and hope. And perhaps here we can return again to Augustine's *Confessions*: modern scholars have pointed out how the verb *confiteor* shifts its meaning constantly in Augustine's prose, so that 'confession' itself unites at least three distinct concerns.[10] 'Confession' is at once the acknowledgment of sin, the proclamation of faith, and the praise of God. In V.1 of the *Confessions* we see the interweaving at work: God is to be offered 'confession' as a sacrifice of praise; confession is the revelation of inner life; but as such it is not *needed* by God (who knows the secrets of the heart), but is offered as witness and exhortation to the world. Confession displays the memory of sin as an occasion for the glorifying of God. This is still further developed in the five opening chapters of Book X, which lead into the profound meditation on memory that crowns the argument. The 'confession' of what Augustine has been and is—the sinner, the penitent, still needy and dependent—is always and fundamentally an oblique 'confession' of God's grace. To know oneself as a reconciled sinner is to know God as a reconciling saviour. Thus, as we penetrate more and more deeply into the mystery of our sense of ourselves, our recollection of a personal history, we see more and more clearly how it is rooted in and surrounded by a more comprehensive mystery—the eternal Truth to whom all things are present. There is a self to remember, to be aware of, because there is an eternal awareness of all events; and to remember a sinful past before God is to apprehend that everlasting awareness as patient, gracious, accepting and transforming.

> Look how I have wandered around in my memory seeking for you, Lord—and indeed it is not outside my memory that I have found you. Since the time I first learned of you, there is nothing of you I have discovered that I have not discovered by remembering. For since that time I have never been unmindful of you. And wherever I found the truth, there I found my God, who is the Truth itself: since learning that truth, I have never been unmindful of it. And so, since that time, you have remained in my memory. There it is that I find you, whenever I recollect you and delight in you.[11]

Thus, if we learn the truth of our selfhood and its history, if we *remember*, and find that that truth can be assimilated in a present experience of gratitude, affirmation, praise, our self-presence involves the presence of God. And the resurrection gospel affirms that this learning and accepting of our past occurs centrally and 'typically' in the presence of the risen Jesus, in the return of the crucified to his crucifiers.

Before even the risen Jesus can be preached to the city which has killed him, he must return to those closest to him (those whose task it will be to preach his good news) and show them *their* part in his death. They had the greatest hopes: theirs, therefore, were the greatest illusions. They must learn the truth of their collusion with the violence which destroyed Jesus, learn that before they can preach to others they must themselves repent and turn—acknowledge their 'identity of failure' before they can again be 'apostles', missionaries.[12]

3

All this suggests one reason for the indispensability in the New Testament of 'apparition stories' in accounts of the resurrection (even in condensed credal formulae like that used by Paul in 1 Cor. 15). The apostles do not simply change their minds and begin preaching: they are *preached to*—by Jesus himself. As they will restore the guilty past to the lords of the council and all the house of Israel in Jerusalem, so their guilty past is first restored; and, obviously and theologically, for them it is only Jesus who can do this, because there is no one else at this stage who can preach. No one else has been through the 'resurrection' process of recovery and grace. And if Paul can later claim that Jesus' appearance to him was on a level with the first apparitions to the Eleven and to James, it is presumably because he cannot recognize that his experience of memory restored in grace owes anything to the preaching of the apostles; he is convicted, just as they were, of collusion in the killing of Jesus simply by the presence of the risen and exalted victim. His exceptional relation of violent hostility to the disciples of Jesus gives his conversion an immediacy comparable only to that of Easter Sunday itself. It may be that his insistence in Gal. 1:15–20 that he learned nothing at this stage from 'flesh and blood', and that he subsequently conferred at Jerusalem only with the two great witnesses, Peter and James, is not merely a defensive ploy to underline his independence of the 'circumcision party', but a reflection of his intense and lasting conviction that he is not a convert like other converts. He is *Christ's* convert, and his alone.[13]

Reading the apparition stories in this light can be instructive. We have seen how these themes suffuse the dialogue with Peter in John 20; but there are other points in the narratives worth observing. The risen Jesus, for instance, *eats* with his disciples—in the Upper Room (Luke 24: 41–3), at Emmaus (ibid., 30–1), at the lakeside (John 21). At the most obvious level, this is a restoration of the memory simply of Jesus' table-fellowship with the disciples during his ministry; but in all the narratives there are both verbal and 'pictorial' echoes of two specific incidents—the feeding of the multitude with bread and fish, and the Last Supper. Now for John at least, the former incident is a crucial one, an occasion of catastrophic misunderstanding (the crowd wish to acclaim Jesus as king, John 6:15), leading into the long meditation on the destiny of the Son of man to be given up 'for the life of the world', to be devoured by a grace-starved humanity; and this discourse itself provokes a crisis of faith, and a rejection of Jesus by 'many' of his followers (John 6:66). The recollection of the Last Supper is more muted (John, after all, has no 'Institution Narrative'), though there may be a fugitive allusion in 21:12 to 16:23a: the unclarity about who or what Jesus is, which is reflected in the pedestrian questioning of the apostles at the Supper is decisively over at Easter—as Jesus has predicted. Luke, however, is more direct: bread is blessed and shared at Emmaus, as at the Supper, and Jesus is recognized in that act. But the Supper is the scene of Peter's protest that he will be faithful, as of Jesus' warning of critical temptation ahead, and his exhortation to Peter to 'strengthen' the apostolic band when he has 'turned again' (Luke 22:31–4). And in response to Jesus' ironic advice to buy a sword for the coming struggle, the apostles proudly display their weapons, provoking Jesus' bitter, 'It is enough' (ibid., 38).

In other words, the resurrection meals, for John and Luke alike, echo specific occasions of crisis, misunderstanding, illusion and disaster. They 'recover' not only the memory of table-fellowship, but the memory of false hope, betrayal and desertion, of a past in which ignorance and pride and the rejection of *Jesus'* account of his destiny in favour of power-fantasies of their own led the disciples into their most tragic failure, their indirect but real share in the ruin of their Lord. Yet Jesus, even as he sees their rejection taking shape, none-theless gives himself to his betrayers in the breaking of bread. The resurrection meals restore precisely that poignant juxtaposition of his unfailing grace and their rejection, distortion and betrayal of it.

We may pause here for a moment to recall that this juxtaposition is built into every Christian celebration of the Eucharist. The narrative of the institution is introduced with a reminder that the sacrament of Jesus' self–gift originates 'in the same night that he was betrayed'. Those who eat at Jesus' table are his betrayers, then as now; yet from the death and hell to which our betrayal condemns him, he returns to break his bread with us as before. The Eucharist is never a simple fellowship meal, not even a simple fellowship meal with Jesus. Its imagery always and necessarily operates between the two poles of Maundy Thursday and Easter Sunday, between Gethsemane and Emmaus, between the Upper Room before the crucifixion and the Upper Room to which the risen Jesus comes. All meals with Jesus after Calvary speak of the *restoration* of a fellowship broken by human infidelity: the wounded body and the shed blood are inescapably present. We do not eucharistically remember a distant meal in Jerusalem, nor even a distant death: we are made 'present to ourselves' as people complicit in the betrayal and death of Jesus and yet still called and accepted, still 'companions' of Christ in the strict sense—those who break bread with him. The Eucharist recapitulates the Supper, the betrayal and the cross, but it does so as an *Easter* feast. Because of the highly concrete nature of what is done, the stress on *present* fellowship, it is a meal like that at Emmaus—never innocent of the memory of Gethsemane and Good Friday, of our illusory hopes and the destruction they unleash when their untruth is manifested, yet never stopping at the stage of shame or even penitence alone. And here is a hint of the theme we shall be exploring in the next chapter, the manner in which the Church's life is a perpetual Easter, and its mission the 'universalizing' of Easter.

The resurrection of Jesus, then, is not simply the raising and the restoration to the world of his past identity (though that is a vital component in the situation, to which we shall return later). Equally importantly, it is the 'raising' of the past identity of those who have been with him. The risen truth shows us the self-deceptions which have drawn us into the vortex of destructiveness. 'Look', says the risen Christ, 'and see that, whatever your hopes and your longings, you were still trapped in fantasy, in blindness to yourselves and to the reality confronting you. Look how you trapped me and handed me over to death. Learn the depth of your resistance to the truth.' And yet the whole of that past that is shared with Jesus is now to be transformed: as we learn the truth of its tragic character, we learn also that the tragedy is interwoven with hope. The truth incarnate, present in the human world, is instantly, inevitably, entangled with the luxuriant tendrils of human fantasy and self-deceit. Throughout the ministry of Jesus, we are reminded of the longing of disciples and 'multitude' alike for a saviour congruent with their projections and aspirations. There is no breaking-free from this web, because entanglement in it is inseparable from human being—the conditions of imperfect knowledge and imperfect communication, combined with the urge to structure and subdue the world and tame its contingency. And thus truth in this world is a stranger, essentially and profoundly vulnerable (so the Fourth Gospel reiterates again and again): its connection with or participation in the world involves rejection, crucifixion outside the city gates. Yet it *has* entered the world, it has allowed itself to be linked with the sphere of destructive untruth; and even if rejected, it cannot be annihilated. If Calvary shows the links between truth and untruth pulling the former down towards extinction, Easter shows us those same links, the same interconnectedness of the human world, reversed, so that truth draws untruth up towards the light. Our connection with truth, with Jesus, has led to the cross; *his* connection with *us* remains, indestructibly, to assure us that our betrayal is not the ultimate fact in the world. We may betray, but the world characterized by betrayal is now interwoven with a reality incapable of betrayal. God's faithfulness has worn a human face, through Calvary and beyond. The incarnate truth, 'risen from the dead', establishes that faithfulness as the ground of inexhaustible hope in the world, even in the midst of our self-deceits.

To know the full scope and the full cost of our untruthfulness, and not to be crippled, paralysed, by it is what is given by the risen Christ: memory restored in hope. St John has Jesus, in the Farewell Discourses, announcing the advent of a Paraclete who will lead the apostles 'into all truth' (15:13), and witness to what 'belongs to' Jesus (ibid. 14), bringing to mind again the work and words of Jesus (14:26). So this unique conjunction of truthfulness and hope in the Christian consciousness which is the Easter gospel is a great part of what we mean by the work of the Spirit. To speak of Jesus as raised 'in Spirit'—designated God's Son 'according to the Spirit of holiness' (Rom. 1:4)—and to identify our share in risen life with our adoption in the Spirit (Rom. 8, *passim*) reflects the same motif. Truthfulness given to human beings and 'sustained' in them, as a constant self-critical, alert, prayerful and receptive turning-back to Jesus, is the gift of the indwelling 'Spirit'. And as given in the resurrection experience, it is also the empowerment to preach and realize the grace of Christ (John 20:22, 23). If we search for the bridge connecting our forgiven-ness with the commission to forgive, it is to be found in the presence with believers of the Spirit, given for recollection of Jesus *and* witness to Jesus. Our identity as restored betrayers, as welcome enemies, is grounded in the present act of God in the Christian community bringing Jesus before the eyes of that community (which is why we need a theology of the Spirit in thinking about the sacraments, and, no less importantly, in thinking about Scripture—less a theology of inspiration 'behind' the text than a theology of Spirit-directed interpretation in the present reading of the text, a theology of the re-presenting of Jesus).

Life in 'Spirit' unites truthfulness and hope. We are given both a past and a future, a *vocation*. That assurance of future

grace is implied in our connectedness with Jesus: as we consciously and deliberately articulate our commitment to 'being
with Jesus', allowing his truth to give us back our past, we
join in the process by which the human 'connectedness' that
is made destructive and treacherous by our self-deceit and
pride becomes saving. We become 'carriers' of the truthfulness of Jesus. The believer who lives in the furnace of this
truth is being made a witness to the rest of humanity of the
possibility of living with truth—burning, but not consumed;
and thus he or she becomes part of God's act of giving back
to the world its memory. In the Spirit, we are not only the
recipients but the transmitters of hope, and our new identity
is bound up with that destiny to transmit hope, to 'preach
the gospel'.

4

All this, of course, implies yet again a point already raised:
God does not come to 'humanity' in the abstract; forgiveness
engages with a particular past. And we can now press this a
stage further, and insist that grace does not create an 'abstract' future: the new identity of life in the Spirit remains
uniquely particular. Paul spells this out in terms of the diversity of the Spirit's gifts (1 Cor. 12:4-30), a vision of com-
plementarity in which common life and particular vocation
do not threaten one another. The new identity is specified in
terms of occupying a unique 'non-transferable' place in the
community, and the community is bonded together by the
communication and exchange between these unique points of
grace-giving. Linking this up with the burden of this chapter
so far, we might say that the community lives in the exchange,
not simply of charisms in Paul's sense, but of *stories*, of memories. My particular past is there, in the Church, as a resource
for my relations with my brothers and sisters—not to be
poured out repeatedly and promiscuously, but as a hinterland
of vision and truth and acceptance, out of which I can begin
to love in honesty. My charism, the gift given me to give to
the community, is my *self*, ultimately; my story given back,

to give me a place in the net of exchange, the web of gifts, which is Christ's Church. My self is to be given away in love, not because it is worthless, but because it is supremely precious, given to me by the hand of God as he returns my memory. Out of my story, the Spirit of the risen Jesus constitutes my present possibilities of understanding, compassion and self-sharing. My identity as lover in the community is uniquely coloured by the loves in which I have already struggled, failed, learned, repented: they are the reason for my present love being in this 'key' or 'mode' rather than that, the irreducible particularity of my gift.

'Love your neighbour as yourself': love in the mode that emerges from the past that is yours and no one else's, out of the process in which you have learned to accept yourself. Begin to see your self as gift, love it as gift, from God's hand, and learn how the neighbour too is a gift, to himself or herself, and to you. In the first chapter, we considered the state of 'fallen' humanity in terms of a chain of mutual deprivation, robbery with violence: here we see how 'redeemed' humanity inverts this system into a chain of mutual gift, exchange of life. And the pivot is the learning of one's own self as gift, allowing it to be returned—whatever the initial pain or shame—by the risen Christ, hearing one's true name from his lips.

'Jesus said to her, "Mary". She turned and said to him in Hebrew, "Rabboni!" (which means Teacher)' (John 20:16). Here, with rare intensity and economy, John unites for us the moments of recognizing (or remembering) self and recognizing (or remembering) God. The crucial instant in which the stranger who appears to have robbed or deprived or diminished ('If you have carried him away . . . .') is revealed as saviour is the utterance of the particular and personal *name.* Mary is offered her name, her identity, the name which specifies her as the person with a particular story. And in this context, the utterance of the name re-establishes a relation of trust and recognition: Mary suddenly sees the stranger as the one who has in the past called her by name, accepted and affirmed her identity. Prior to this, it is not simply the Lord's body that has been carried away—it is the Lord who has

loved and affirmed Mary, and so, in a sense, it is Mary herself
who has been 'carried away'. Nothing here of the themes of
betrayal and illusion permeating the Peter stories (it is important for the evangelist, as we shall see later, that Mary
does *not* belong to the apostolic band who deserted Jesus in
his passion): only the most basic and naked sense of loss,
need, void, prior even to the sense of guilt or failure.[14]

> About women, no one can know. There are some,
> Like this one, whose pain is a locked sepulchre;
> Their pain is buried in them, there is no fleeing
> From it and no casting it off . . .
> . . . Deep calls unto deep, a grave for a grave,
> A carcass drawing towards a carcass in that unhappy
>   morning;
> Three days was this one in a grave, in a world that died
> In the cry in the afternoon. It is finished,
> The cry that drew blood from her like the barb of a sword.
> It is finished. Finished. Mary fell from the hill
> To the emptiness of the last Easter . . . .
> A world without a living Christ, the horrifying Sabbath of
>   creation,
> The abyss of the hundred thousand centuries and their
>   end,
> Mary lay down in the grave of the trembling universe.
> . . . All the flowers of memory withered except the rain of
>   blood
> . . . God was extinguished,
> In the dying together, in the burying together . . . .[15]

Whatever there is of complicity in the Lord's death is
irrelevant: that can be dealt with later. Here we are back
again in the world sketched in the first chapter, the world of
dead souls, victim and oppressor alike. The 'Sabbath of creation', the grave of self is what is before us, the death of the
sense of being valued, being loved, being given a *place*: to the
dead Christ comes the robbed self. The beginnings of restoration and affirmation have been stirred (Mary, remember,
has been exorcized by Jesus—John surely assumes that much
knowledge of who Magdalene is), but the hope of the early

days is challenged and broken in the cross, the unveiling of the heart's darkness. And we are twice dead when Jesus dies, for this is the death—or near-death—of hope.

But if hope, mortally wounded, is still capable of turning back to the abandoned body, there is still a discovery to be made. Mary has already 'turned back' to the tomb, returning after Calvary; finding it empty, she tells the apostles of this— surely final?—blow to hope and peace, yet returns again; and back at the grave, she turns (v. 14) to see a stranger whom she fails to recognize. But when he addresses her by name, she 'turns' one last time to recognition: *s t r a p h e i s a ekeine legei auto(i) Ebraisti, Rabbounei* (16)—she, 'having turned', she, 'the one who had turned', again and again, in ever-dwindling hope, now finds that hope answered. Turning, over and again, to the name, the figure, the recollection of Jesus, even when it can only seem abstract and remote, issues at last in knowing with utter clarity that it is still he who calls us into our unique identity. Jesus is 'lost' by our betrayal, or simply 'lost' as we are carried away from him in the violent turmoil of the human world; whether by sin or by suffering (to use the conventional categories), our value and our self-love is lost with him. But conversion, the turning of *metanoia*, the repentance of which the New Testament speaks, is the refusal to accept that lost-ness is the final human truth. Like a growing thing beneath the earth, we protest at the darkness and push blindly up in search of light, truth, *home*—the place, the relation where we are not lost, where we can live from deep roots in assurance. Mary goes blindly back to the tomb, and finds her self, her home, her name; her protest, her dissatisfaction with dissat-isfaction, is decisively vindicated. Mary is not dead because Jesus is not dead. 'I will not leave you desolate. I will come to you. Yet a little while, and the world will see me no more, but you will see me; *because I live, you will live also*' (John 14:18–19).

Mary lives because Jesus lives; her conversion is the event of recognition that occurs when her protest is met with re-sponse. And her 'sanctification', her growth in converted life, will have to do with the *daily* refusal to accept that lost, 'deprived' humanity can simply be lived with or shrugged off.

Growth is in the passionate constancy of returning to what seems a grave, a void, to the dim recollection of a possibility of love, in the hope of hearing one's name spoken out of the emptiness. 'Deep calls unto deep': not simply the buried Jesus calling the buried self into a shared tomb, but the inexhaustible depth of God's remembering love calling to the depth of hope and potentiality and freedom in the self. If we answer that call, and find our story given back to us, our name and our memory, that story turns the corner into life and promise, and, most importantly, 'calling' in the fuller sense. We are given a task to do, given a gift to give. Mary is bidden not to touch or hold or cling to the recovered Lord, 'but go to my brethren and say to them, I am ascending to my Father and your Father' (John 20:17). The resurrection stories, as we have noted, lead invariably into a commissioning: the word of hope is given to be passed on, from Mary to the apostles, from the Ten to Thomas, from Peter to the flock he must tend; from the whole community to the whole world. 'All authority in heaven and on earth has been given to me. Go therefore and make disciples of all nations' (Matt. 28:18–19).

But to communicate that word involves some measure of sensitivity to the dimension of search and protest in one another and in the world at large.[16] The resurrection is not properly preached without an awareness of the human world as a place of loss and a place where men and women strive not to be trapped in that loss. The 'converted' apostle preaches to, and in the middle of, this experience, and is constrained to see the beginning of conversion in every turning-away from the dead acceptance of loss. The world is a place of incipient conversion, in its restlessness and in its struggle for a truth and a home, for justice, restoration, fulfilment. Where men and women recognize truthfully the reality of pain, deprivation and oppression in the world (and in their own lives), and react with passion and engagement, they have turned into the void of lostness in a kind of unspoken, unformulable hope. And it may on occasion take forms barely recognizable as hope. Here is a story of such a problematic act—from Ulster, so much a touchstone for the honesty of religious or moral schemes. A mother noticed that her teenage son was in obvious distress and fear; when questioned, he admitted that he was involved with a (Protestant) para-military group, which had ordered him to perform a killing locally, or else face 'execution' himself. The mother was able to say eventually that being killed was preferable to killing; that night, her son hanged himself.

Despair or not? At one level, obviously, despair, the sense that there is no way out of the nightmare; yet also a passionate refusal of the terms in which the options had been presented, a protest. Here is a person who sees clearly that the world he is part of is intolerable; he will not go on abusing his own humanity by colluding with what that world prescribes. In other circumstances, there might be a form of creative protest that could be made. For a working-class youth in Belfast, there might well seem no protest possible except suicide. But, as an act of refusal, an act fiercely protesting against collusion with the world's violence, it is, I would presume to say, a *converted* act—so tragically, so obscurely, as to be barely intelligible as such, yet within the appalling confines of the situation, as felt and seen by the victim, still a statement that the human world is not-at-home, estranged, 'improper', when it closes itself up in threats and murder. And the one who has thus 'turned' in refusal from a trapped world may indeed be turning to hear his or her name spoken by the Lord.

As I have said, there are more creative protests; but the point is that we learn to see the meaningfulness of such converted protest even where it is without any obvious resources of power and effectiveness. Protest affirms the hope that there is a name for the nameless, a face for the lost: good news for the poor. Here the resurrection gospel speaks of the proper expectation—the *right*—of all men and women to responsible identity, the capacity to be self-aware agents empowered to take active part in the 'net of exchange'. The 'saved' man or woman is one with sufficient sense of his or her dignity, selfhood and resourcefulness to love generously. To such people, the restoration of self, in the sense of the restoration of a story, a memory, a hinterland to the present and a perspective upon it, is indeed a vocation to pursue the building of a world in which this right is fully realized. These

first two chapters have attempted to show how the Christian
proclamation of the resurrection of the crucified just man, his
return to his unfaithful friends and his empowering of them
to forgive in his name offers a narrative structure in which
we can locate our recovery of identity and human possibility,
a paradigm of the 'saving' process; yet not only a paradigm.
It is a story which is itself an indispensable *agent* in the
completion of this process, because it witnesses to the one
personal agent in whose presence we may have full courage
to 'own' ourselves as sinners and full hope for a humanity
whose identity is grounded in a recognition and affirmation
by nothing less than God. It is a story which makes possible
the comprehensive act of *trust* without which growth is
impossible.

Every human life lived in self-awareness and hopefulness
is in some measure a conquest of the threat of lostness and
imprisoning guilt. But we tell the story of Jesus as the record
of a life which not only embodied gift, meaning and freedom
is a unique and definitive way, but also was crowned by a
strange and elusive event which declared this life not to be
over. This human life is declared to be God's, to belong with
God; that is, it is shown to share in the radical creative energy
that generates all things. Thus its meaningfulness is not restricted by historical circumstance. Cornelius Ernst has well
said[17] that every human struggle after meaning is the process
'by which the world to which man belongs becomes the world
which belongs to man': a meaningful life is a 'metaphor', a
transformation of the world's meaning. Thus, he continues,
the resurrection, as the crown of a supremely meaningful life,
is the ultimate 'metaphor': 'In the Resurrection, the world
which belongs to man becomes the world which belongs to
God.' So, to believe in the risen Jesus is to trust that the
generative power of God is active in the human world; that
it can be experienced as transformation and recreation and
empowerment in the present; and that its availability and
relevance extends to every human situation.

The community of faith, the community which lives by
exchange and gift in its relation to Jesus and to itself, is
charged with sharing this vision and this possibility of life

with all the world (Matt 28:19, Mark 16:15, Luke 24:42; Acts 1:8). We need to look next at the way in which the Church as a community speaks to the human community at large, in its life and structures, its ritual and its conscious attempts at evangelism. How does the universal possibility begin to become *actually* universal? How does the restored and 'rehumanized' Church respond to its vocation to join in God's creation of a world imaging his own life?

Notes

1. For discussion of the weaknesses of such a model, see, e.g., Iris Murdoch, *The Sovereignty of Good*, (RKP 1970); and Thomas Nagel, *Mortal Questions* (CUP 1979), pp. 196–9.
2. See the chapter on 'Memory' in Johann-Baptist Metz's *Faith in History and Society* (Burns & Oates 1980).
3. This was plainly articulated in the message sent by the Zimbabwe churches to the 1980 World Conference on Mission and Evangelism held in Melbourne; see the Report of this conference, *Your Kingdom Come. Mission Perspectives* (WCC, Geneva, 1980), p. 237.
4. J.-B. Metz, op. cit., p. 195.
5. Ibid., p. 193.
6. See especially *Confessions*, X. 17. This is finely discussed by J.-M. Le Blond, *Les conversions de Saint Augustin* (Aubier, Paris, 1950), pp. 181ff; and cf. Ray S. Anderson, *Historical Transcendence and the Reality of God* (Geoffrey Chapman 1975), p. 19, n 66, on Kierkegaard's account of 'spirit' as 'presence to myself'.
7. 'Abram Tertz' (Andrei Sinyavsky), in his letters to his wife from a Soviet labour camp, illustrates this kind of recovery very vividly, writing not only about the rich traditional Christian culture of peasant Russia, but also about the curious, vigorous, highly ritualized and formulaic language and thought-world of the thieves and gangsters in the camps; see the selection from his letters published as *A Voice from the Chorus* (Collins & Harvill 1976).
8. See D. M. MacKinnon, 'Some Notes on the Irreversibility of Time', in *Explorations in Theology* 5 (SCM 1979), pp. 90–8, especially pp. 96–7.
9. See Gerald O' Collins, s. j., *The Easter Jesus* (DLT 1973), p. 23: 'In the first gospel . . . it is natural to find Jesus separating himself from the unbelieving city. . . . Revelation no longer makes Jerusalem its centre, but has moved from there to Galilee and will move from Galilee out to the rest of mankind.'

10. See especially P. Courcelle, *Recherches sur les 'Confessions' de saint Augustin* (Paris, Boccard, 1950), pp. 13ff.

11. *Confessions* X. 24.

12. See the brilliant discussion of this theme in Edward Schillebeeckx's *Jesus. An Experiment in Christology* (Collins 1979), pp. 381ff.

13. It is tempting to suggest that the problematic phrase, 'I belong to Christ' in 1 Cor. 1:12, should indeed be put into Paul's own mouth (as some exegetes have suggested), and be read as meaning, 'I, Paul, am *directly* Christ's convert—as some are Cephas' or Apollos' '. Paul is reminding his readers that all true apostolic authority refers *immediately* to the one Christ, so that there can be no divisive 'personality cults' in the Church.

14. Sebastian Moore, in *The Fire and the Rose Are One* (DLT 1980), attempts to broaden and correct the perspective of his earlier book by concentrating less on 'generic guilt' and more on the fundamental need for loving recognition by the 'other': this is something of the shift in emphasis I am trying to express here.

15. Saunders Lewis, 'Mary Magdalene' (tr. from the Welsh by Gwyn Thomas), in Alun R. Jones and Gwyn Thomas, ed., *Presenting Saunders Lewis*, (Cardiff, University of Wales Press, 1973), pp. 191–3.

16. Raymond Fung, of the Hong Kong Christian Council, has insisted that evangelism must begin from a sensitivity to human 'sinned-against-ness', and thus from solidarity with the lost and the violated, rather than from a preoccupation with sinfulness as such. The contrast is perhaps overdrawn, but the point is a valid one; see his moving and cogent 'Good News to the Poor—A Case for a Missionary Movement', in *Your Kingdom Come*, pp. 83–92.

17. F. Kerr and T. Radcliffe, ed., *Multiple Echo* (DLT 1979), p. 75.

CHAPTER THREE

Communities of Resurrection

1

The recovery of the past in the forgiving presence of Jesus is a vocation and a commission. We have learned to live by gift; to us is entrusted the vision of a humanity liberated from fear and shame by the gift of God's presence in the risen Jesus. And this liberation is not a bland legitimation of all we are and do, despite the fact that it involves an *acceptance* of what we are. Forgiveness does not occur without the reality of that relation and transaction in which we discover the victim as saviour; it does not occur without that transcendence of violent and oppressive models of relationship discussed in our first chapter. So to live a 'forgiven' life is not simply to live in a happy consciousness of having been absolved. Forgiveness is precisely the deep and abiding sense of what relation— with God or with other human beings—can and should be; and so it is itself a stimulus, an irritant, necessarily provoking protest at impoverished versions of social and personal relations. Once we grasp that forgiveness occurs not by a word of acquittal but by a transformation of the world of persons, we are not likely to regard it as something which merely refers backwards.

And so the Spirit in whose power sins are to be forgiven (John 20:22–3), the counsellor and companion of the believing community (John 14:16ff), is also a Spirit of judgement and

52

discernment (John 16:8–11), a Spirit of truthfulness. We have seen (in the last chapter) how the Spirit keeps alive in us the possibility of turning back in hope to Jesus and his truthfulness. And in this light we can properly speak of the Spirit's work in terms of discrimination, even 'convicting', as we read in St John. In the Spirit, judgement is *constantly* to be pronounced upon 'the prince of this world', the dominant destructiveness in unredeemed human relations. It is not pronounced in isolated prophetic utterance: that model of the activity of 'Spirit' belongs to an older and less nuanced tradition.[1] Instead it is pronounced in the characteristic life of the believing community. Just as Jesus himself embodies but does not pronounce the world's judgement (that favourite theme of St John), so with the Church (John 15:18—16:4), which is thus liable to the same rejection. The difference is that the Church does this only because of its own self-critical awareness, its turning to the truthfulness of Jesus: it has no truthfulness but his, just as it has no holiness but his ('Sanctify them in thy truth', Jesus prays in John 17:17).

The Church's work of judgement, its critical role in the world, is a nonsense (and worse) if criticism is not built into its own life and structures. Only a penitent Church can manifest forgiven-ness—a tautology, perhaps, but worth saying. A merely critical Church can reproduce in horrifying forms precisely those oppressive and exclusive relations which it exists to judge. It will pass sentence upon those beyond its boundaries, and so will be concerned about those boundaries and their exact definition. It will, explicitly or implicitly, see 'belonging to the Church' as a matter of fulfilling conditions of membership; so that it possesses criteria by which some believers can be cut off when necessary from its life. It thus encourages that attitude between believers or groups of believers which is almost preternaturally alert to failure and delinquency. I am not speaking simply of certain kinds of Irish Catholicism or Welsh Nonconformity (such as have been immortalized by James Joyce or Caradoc Evans); soi-distant 'radical' Christianity is capable of the same level of pharisaism. The former Archbishop of Cape Town has written searchingly of the temptation, in a situation of acute political strain and conflict, to 'bludgeon' the opposition with accusations designed to engender guilt rather than (in the widest sense) conversion, and converted action.[2] The exposed situation of the prophetic or protesting group often seems to require for its security the firm projection of guilt on to the dissident or lukewarm; and any sense of judgement and grace or hope flowing together from the awareness of forgiven-ness in the prophetic group is pretty elusive.

This is not a plea for that ecclesiastical blandness incapable of making enemies which characterizes so much of our church life. The Church has constantly to risk causing hurt and offence ('Every moral problem of the slightest interest is a problem about who is to get hurt').[3] But so often, prophecy and protest are conceived as essentially a message to be articulated, with little attention paid to the roots of that 'message' (a near-useless word in this context) in the form of shared life and the style of self-awareness which distinguishes a 'believing' community, a community which trusts God and itself enough to live in honesty and acceptance. Prophecy which flows from such a centre is authentically a form of non-violent resistance: non-violent, because it does not aim simply to identify and locate blame so that it can condemn, exclude, and disparage; but resistance because it speaks of a drastic *refusal* of certain styles of individual and corporate life—a refusal which encompasses the whole of the prophet's existence. We can see especially clearly in Jeremiah, Ezekiel and (probably) Hosea how the prophet's life itself becomes the sign communicating God's judgement to Israel. But more evident still is the element of resistance in the monastic movement in the fourth and fifth Christian centuries: the religious life, especially in its solitary forms, refuses to identify 'being a Christian' with belonging to a Christian family or a Christian society. The believing life can be lived without kin and without citizenship; if they disappear, belief need not.

Such a witness is, of course, a caveat for the rest of the Church rather than a judgement. More to the point, perhaps, are those communities deliberately created in response to an overwhelming failure in the society around—multi-racial 'cells' in a racist society,[4] or communities in which the disabled, the mentally and physically handicapped or the marginal are accorded a place of worth and security, put in a position where they are enabled to have the dignity of giving as well as receiving (Jean Vanier's 'L'Arche' communities illustrate this ideal most profoundly and forcefully).[5] Such groups judge very eloquently; they do not merely speak of possible transformations, but enact them. And to be able to participate in a community of this kind requires the recognition that I am myself deprived and diminished when I cannot receive the gifts that a person of another culture or colour, or a spastic, or a vagrant, or an ex-prisoner can give—and also that if I collude with this diminution by a refusal to engage, I am forging the chains of active sin. This recognition builds into the life of a group the dimension of self-critical awareness, the 'constructive suspicion' of one's liability to reject and deny. We might even speak of a kind of penitence involved in the acknowledgement that there has been in the past an individual or a societal collusion with the state of mutual isolation and privation which locks away the disabled, 'abnormal' and unacceptable.

But these are only vivid images of the Church—clearly-defined fragments of 'church-like' living in areas of human experience where division is especially sharp and tragic. Belief in Christ involves (if our discussion has been on the right lines thus far) a vision of the entire human world as a network of oppression and privation, in which no one is wholly free from the responsibility of making victims: so that penitent awareness is indispensably part of reconstructed humanity. The community (like L'Arche) whose aim is to speak to one particular area of mutual isolation may show elements of penitence, but that is not unequivocally part of its very nature. The Church, however, addresses itself to all human violence, *in* all human beings. If it is to be itself, it has no option but to live in penitence, in critical self-awareness and acknowledgement of failure. It must recognize constantly its failing *as* a community to *be* a community of gift and mutuality, and warn itself of the possibility of failure.

What kind of gospel can plausibly be preached, for instance, by a Church which is unable to deal with the moral, emotional or psychological collapse of one of its ministers except by a mixture of frigid and embarrassed public silence and punitive internal discipline? It is not often that we hear leaders of our churches—it is not often that we hear *any* of us—admitting in such cases the failure of a community to love its ministers pastorally and the breakdown of mutual support between clergy; or warmly assuring the victim not only of the Church's love and forgiveness but of its willingness to learn from them, to receive some challenge, enlargement, even enrichment from their trust and hope. Yet all this is part of what it is to be a penitent Church—to say as firmly as possible that no one's failure is theirs alone, and that no failure can put an end to the relation of mutual gift that is the ground of the community's life. Historic Christianity has, of course, disciplined believers by means of excommunication; but we should remember that, primitively, excommunication (so far from excluding the sinner wholly from the Church) accorded the recognized status of a penitent *within* the Church.[6] It was a recognition that the bonds of communal life (so much stronger in the early Church than today) were ruptured by sin, and its orientation was towards reconciliation (sometimes only in the next world, but nonetheless reconciliation). Whatever the strengths and weaknesses of this sort of discipline, we have to admit that (at least in 'North Atlantic' Christendom) we have nothing to correspond to this: excommunication has far too long been simply a penalty, absolving the community from any active work of restoring relations. We cannot use the traditional acceptability of such a practice to modify the Church's vocation to preserve the sinner's place in the community.

Another obvious area in which Christian communities are slow to show themselves as penitent is the world of inter-Church relations. Most Christian bodies have, at one point or another, exercised some degree of violence towards each other; and this is remembered most vividly in the celebration of martyrs. Now the memory of the martyr is an extraordinarily potent thing, and it can be used as a most effective instrument of repression, internally (it is unthinkable to modify the faith or liturgy for which the martyrs shed their blood) and externally (it is unthinkable to come to any accommodation with those by whom the martyrs' blood was shed). But if Christian belief expresses itself in communities of gift, there must be the possibility of the martyr's death becoming a 'gift' to the martyr's murderers, the persecuted group becoming a 'gift' to its enemies. And this requires two things: that the martyr's community celebrate the martyr's memory in such a way that he or she offers grace and hope to those outside; and that the persecuting body remember the martyr in penitence and thanksgiving. Now that the Church of England celebrates Thomas More, George Fox and John Bunyan in its calendar, we begin to see a little of what this might involve; but the network still has a long way to spread. And celebration of this kind, we should note, does not involve an unweaving of history or a recantation of disagreements: what is celebrated is witness and sacrifice, and the hope must be that the martyr's generous love can fertilize even the fiery drought of the persecutors' hearts.

In short, the martyr dies in an affirmation of God's lordship—the affirmation that God is the ultimate value to be loved and served. He or she dies 'in Christ'; for Christ is the voice and face in history of that lordship. And so the martyr is exalted with Christ, shares the risenness of Jesus, and thus becomes part of the ceaseless gift of grace and acceptance that Christ pours out to the world. To celebrate *any* Christian martyr is to celebrate the resurrection: so to make of the martyr a weapon against others is an offence against the resurrection faith, and to make of one's *own* past of suffering a weapon is no less so.

Thus a major part of the process of reconciliation within the Church is the recovery of the memory of martyrs in a way that is authentically hopeful. It is too easy to allow embarrassment to blot out the vividness of such a memory: the Roman Catholic Church *needs* to remind the Anglican Church of the memory of More, Campion, Southwell, and the rest, just as the Anglican Church *needs* to remind the Roman Church of Latimer and the other victims of Mary Tudor, because the whole Church needs for its wholeness the memory both of its capacity for violence and of the great witnesses to the risen Jesus who have appeared in the midst of it. Paul was not able to forget that he had persecuted the Church of God; but that was for him invariably and inseparably a re- collection of the grace given to him, never an occasion of self-loathing and despair. All Christians have the calling to help their brothers and sisters to a creative and hopeful pen- itence, just as they themselves are bound to be open to the aid of those brothers and sisters in discovering this penitence in their own lives.

We have noted already that the Eucharist is a reminder to the whole Church of its liability to desert and betray: the eucharistic Church 'locates' itself in Gethsemane before it finds itself finally in and with the risen Jesus. Thus the mem- ory of the martyrs (*all* the martyrs) can and should be for the Church a part of its eucharistic life, where it identifies itself as oppressor and traitor, yet also the penitent and restored kin of Christ. When the Church lives 'eucharistically' in this sense, we can once again speak of an eloquent proclaiming of the resurrection gospel to the world. A Church which is not only divided but cements its dividing walls with the blood of the martyrs cannot but be a stumbling-block for the faith of humanity at large: it fails to show forgiven-ness as a style of living. This should make very plain to us the indispensability within the Church not merely of a mentality of self-criticism and penitence, but of *signs* which continually impress on the Church that it is called to penitence. To say that the Eucharist is fundamental to the Church's life is not to say simply that it is 'very useful', nor to say that it is a quasi-physical fuel for the life of the soul. The extremes of internalization (the Eucharist as illustration of a doctrinal point) and deperson- alization (the Eucharist as the confection of a life-giving sub- stance) are equally inadequate. Rather, when the Church performs the eucharistic action it *is* what it is called to be: the Easter community, guilty and restored, the gathering of those whose identity is defined by their new relation to Jesus crucified and raised, who identify themselves as forgiven. What happens in the Eucharist is, among much else, that the Church assembles simply to make this identification in praise and gratitude, and to show in concrete form its dependence on Christ. It is an action which announces what the community's life *means*, where the roots of its understanding and its possibilities are; and as such it is a transforming, a re-creative act—a human activity radically open to the creative activity of God in Jesus.

This is how the sacraments of the Church and the human, relational life of the Church must be held together. The sacramental act identifies the Church, the whole community, by articulating where it is that the Church looks for the sources of its life and understanding: it is a sort of 'taking cognizance' of why the Church strives to live thus and not otherwise.[7] It allows the source-event, the mystery of cross and resurrection, to become present again, and so opens itself to the rich resource of that event. Every sacrament is a sharing in Easter, in the paschal mystery. And in this light, we shall turn next to consider the way in which baptism, the sacrament of entry into the community, expresses all this comprehensively, remembering that this, at least as much as the Eucharist, is very specially an Easter event.

2

Just as the commission to preach forgiveness to all is most unambiguously given in the post-Easter period, so, in Matthew's Gospel, is the command to baptize. 'Go therefore and make disciples of all nations, baptizing them in the name of the Father and of the Son and of the Holy Spirit' (Matt. 28:19). And further, for Matthew, this command is a consequence of Jesus' new status, as the one who possesses 'all authority in heaven and on earth'. There is nowhere, in heaven or on earth, where Jesus cannot be; there is no creature incapable of coming into relation with him. All may be disciples, and all may be baptized in the 'name'—in the power, in the significance—of the threefold divine agency, the source and maker of all, the mediator who does his will, and the Spirit who empowers believers to do that will.

What theology of baptism underlies this command as Matthew records it is unclear. It is Paul who first spells out the connection between baptism and the paschal event in plain terms (Rom. 6:3ff, and possibly 1 Cor. 10:1–4), and there is little to suggest that Matthew was aware of any such clearly-drawn link. Yet if the threefold name indicates, as I have suggested, a reference to Jesus as the Son who pleases God in all things (and thus harks back to the story of Jesus' own baptism in Mark 1:9–11 and parallels), and if the passion of Jesus is the culmination of this pleasing obedience of Son to Father, the connection is not so far to seek. Jesus himself is remembered in the Synoptic tradition as having referred to his death as a 'baptism' (Mark 10:38–39, and parallels), which his followers may be called upon to share, and Luke points this up still further, when he records Jesus' longing to 'accomplish' his baptism of death (12:50). We may not have here a clear 'Pauline' statement that to be baptized is to die and be raised with Christ, but we do have an unmistakeable baptismal metaphor for the culmination of Jesus' mission. Jesus' immersion in the water of John's baptism was, for the first Christians, and almost certainly for Jesus himself, an occasion on which his vocation to total self-gift to the Father became luminously evident to him: it was a kind of consecration or anointing. So it is not strange that he should speak of the costly expression of this self-gift in just such terms of 'immersion': each step in the fulfilment of his vocation is a deepening of this baptism. As the liturgical and pictorial tradition of Eastern Christianity insists, his baptism is a descent ever further into the waters of chaos out of which the descending Spirit will bring a world to birth.[8]

The pivotal point is this: death is normally a drastic severing of relations, death *isolates*; but for Jesus, it is through death that a new and potentially infinite network of relations is opened up. The effect of his death is the opposite of isolation. Thus, if Jesus speaks of his death as a 'baptism', it is natural that those drawn together by his death and exaltation express their reconciliation, their oneness with God and each other in a rite of baptismal immersion. I am not suggesting that the development of a baptismal rite was a deliberate symbolic creation in response to this theological vision: it is quite likely that the first Christians unreflectively continued

the Jewish practice of initiating converts by a rite of purifi-
catory bathing (perhaps encouraged by the word or example
of Jesus: John 4:1–3, despite its confusions, suggests this
strongly),[9] and only gradually linked it with Jesus' language
about his death. But however this occurred, it is plain enough
that, as Jesus' death came to be seen as the source of a new
shared life, the means by which this newness was to be ap-
propriated crystallized as the baptismal rite. Jesus, when he
has passed through death, is restored to the world as the
place and name in which any and every human being may
find grace and hope and identity. His risen presence impels
the disciples to make more disciples—more men and women
who recover their life and their value in that presence. And
to be a disciple, to be with Jesus, is to be baptized: baptism
is the way in which each person is made present to Jesus,
crucified and alive, by a ritual act which places the person in
the same process that Jesus described as 'immersion', the
process of self-forgetting that leads to the cross. Forget you
have a self to be shielded, reinforced, consoled and lied to:
hear the bitter truth that the cross enunciates, and accept the
pain and disorientation of that enlightenment, in the trust
that you are not hated or abandoned; and come up from the
flood with a new person, 'alive to God', living with your eyes
set firmly on the ground and goal of hope which is Jesus. The
believer is not now separable from Jesus—that presence so
defines his or her identity (Rom. 8:9–17, 31–9): we live in the
Spirit of truthfulness, and can truthfully call God 'Abba,
Father'. We know God not only as the one who gives us
being, but as the one who affirms that being. The trust and
hope of Jesus is made ours.

Jesus, we have said, is not isolated by his death, and he
will never die again (Rom. 6:9): there will be no cutting-off
of relation with him (except by our own refusal to be related,
our unwillingness to accept his presence). He is 'dead' to sin
in the sense that he is isolated, separated, only from the
system of destructive violence in which the world is caught:
he is free from the trap of guilt, oppression and fear. Jesus of
Nazareth, as a particular human being with mental and physical limitations, circumscribed by a 'given' world, had shown

in those confines what was involved in a life of non-violence, had lived so as to diminish or reject no one; and God, in raising him, has said, 'This is *my* work, *my* life: what is done in Jesus is what I do, now and always.' The knowledge that Jesus is with God is the knowledge that his life has broken its historical boundaries; it is not limited by the set of relationships within which it was lived in the first century. It is a life which can weave itself into the fabric of lives remote in time and space from its original context—not simply as a narrative memory, but as an active and transforming presence, never exhausted or assimilated. The risen Christ is not a resuscitated human *individual*;[10] he is encountered as a particular historical subject, certainly, in the records of past events, but the work he now performs in our lives cannot be understood in terms of what a human individual, past or present, might do. He never belongs to the past in the sense that what he does or is is over, completed and sealed off. And he does not act in the present simply by influence and example: as we have seen, it is in *confrontation* with his presence that human lives are restored and reshaped.

The Church is part of what that confrontation implies. The challenging and saving presence of Jesus may be encountered in many places—wherever authentic and creative forgiveness occurs and is seen to occur. But the Church is able to say explicitly where this forgiveness has its source, what it is that definitively interprets and locates forgiveness: the resurrection of the crucified. What the believer says is, 'I live because of Jesus, in Jesus. The person I am cannot be understood apart from Jesus. I am baptized: I received my name, my identity, in the process of immersion in the Easter event.' Thus the believer's life is a testimony to the risen-ness of Jesus: he or she demonstrates that Jesus is not dead by living a life in which Jesus is the never-failing source of affirmation, challenge, enrichment and enlargement—a pattern, a dance, intelligible *as* a pattern only when its pivot and heart become manifest. The believer shows Jesus as the centre of his or her life. And because that life is shared, because it is essentially, not accidentally, a life of mutuality, that system of relationships which makes up the community of the baptized testifies equally to the presence of Christ. As Paul Ricoeur has insisted,[11] testimony and *manifestation* belong together: in the 'testimony' of a life-commitment, that which is witnessed to declares or shows itself, becomes manifest as a comprehensive and unconditional source of meaning. The believing community manifests the risen Christ: it does not simply talk about him, or even 'celebrate' him. It is the place where he is shown.[12]

And the baptismal rite imprints upon the believer the mark of Easter, committing this or that particular human life to manifesting Jesus killed and raised. The believer, and thus the *community* of belief, is charged with actualizing in any and every circumstance the Easter transaction, the Easter restoration. There is no alibi for the Church. Jesus, exalted to God's throne, is *already* Lord and King, already the context of understanding and the ground of hope throughout the world: the fact of his exaltation is what stirs the Church to 'mission'. His lordship, the fact that God's 'Kingdom' is his too, is what makes the Church catholic by drawing it further and further into the world. The Kingdom, mission and catholicity cannot be understood apart from each other. All kinds of distortions are liable to arise if these ideas are divorced. The 'Kingdom' can be identified with the visible Church, and treated in terms of fully realized human dominion and authority;[13] 'mission' can be seen as an exercise in communicating information from those who possess it to those who do not (and Christian worship too can, in this perspective, be reduced to an exercise in the clear communication of propositions);[14] 'catholicity' can be interpreted as numerical magnitude, geographical universality, or even theological comprehensiveness. But when these concepts are drawn together, it is possible to see how both catholicity and mission are dimensions of the Church's form of life, a life endlessly sensitive, contemplatively alert to human personal and cultural diversity, tirelessly seeking new horizons in its own experience and understanding by engaging with this diversity, searching to see how the gospel is to be lived and confessed in new and unfamiliar situations; and doing this because of its conviction that each fresh situation is already within the ambience of Jesus' cross and resurrection, open to his agency, under his kingship.

Thus the Romanian theologian Nicolae Chitescu can write:

> [The Church's] relation with the world is an essential factor. . . . The restoration of an external world without barriers of race, language and nationality contributes to the proclamation of truth and catholicity. Thus the Church realizes its catholicity more and more, being the 'home' to all those outside, to those of any human condition, while realizing the gifts of the Holy Spirit in its very being.[15]

Catholicity and mission include not only the work of inter-faith dialogue, or the encounter with Marxism: the work of Mother Teresa, of a 'Life' group concerned with unwanted children, of the Cyrenians serving the needs of vagrant alcoholics, of Christian involvement in a pressure group publicizing the sufferings of Eritrean peasants or Tamil workers, or any other of the less 'fashionable' persecuted nations and races of the world—all this is both catholic and missionary, because it strives to show, to embody, the way in which the incalculable variety of human concerns can be 'at home' in and with the confession of faith in Jesus. It does not seek to impose a uniform Christian culture or a preconceived Christian solution: it aims only to keep open and expanding the frontiers of the community of gift.

The vocation to catholicity is thus uttered to every believing community, however small and localized: each local church is 'catholic', if it is true to its commission.[16] It must be catholic in its range and depth of human concern, in being an environment in which projects of human healing and fulfilment may be at home. But it must be catholic also in its openness to the range and depth of the whole family of believers, past and present: tradition belongs with catholicity, and the rejection of the Christian past creates as many problems as any other kind of rejection. There are features of every church's past (as we have already observed in this chapter) which we cannot affirm or condone; there may be aspects of the theology and devotion of the Church in past ages which are remote, empty, or even repellent. Yet the present Church inherits this past, and must remember it, even if in penitence or puzzlement. 'It is possible to be a believer and yet think that or do that': such must be our alertness to the odd or the unattractive in the Church. It is a sharp reminder of the non-uniformity of 'Christian culture', and may be an aid to flexibility and detachment now. It is also an admission of a kind of responsibility shared with Christians we believe to be wrong—a way of feeling the *hurt* of the Body of Christ, rather than simply lopping off what seems to be a diseased limb.

We, and our opinions and perspectives, do not dictate what the Church is now and certainly not what it has been; and the experience of this loss of control is itself salutary. We are not the hub, the spring of significance, the norm of interpretation in the Church, and neither is any other one segment of the Body. The Church was clearly blasphemously wrong for the greater part of two millennia on the subject of slavery; many would add that it has been no less wrong for even longer about the status of women. To be 'catholic' now involves resisting the temptation to blot out and forget this past, and the equally powerful temptation to condemn from a superior vantage-point. This kind of catholicity obliges us to recognize the Church's fallibility and to admit our complicity in the Church's continuing liability to failure and betrayal. And it does not in any sense weaken the clarity of a present conviction that to live as a believer is, crudely and practically, incompatible with a life-form that takes slavery (or female subjugation) for granted. We cannot live thus; this is where we have been led; and it is impossible not to interpret it as an expansion of the Church's heart, a deepening of the 'catholic' sense. We can only be grateful that even a slave-owning Church had just enough sensitivity to the challenge of the gospel for a protest to be generated (however slowly) and a new awareness—of which we are the direct beneficiaries—to come into being. This is a catholicity which may weep over the universal liability to error, yet rejoice at the universal pressure towards truth, penitence and transformation. We belong to a community doubly vulnerable: to self-deceit, and to the unremitting leavening of the truth proclaimed in word and sacrament. Our openness to the polychromatic ambiguity of the Church's history can teach us that at least.

This may help us to understand something of why the Church's historic ordained ministry has been seen as a guardian tradition. The ministry's continuity with itself in time and space makes it a major sign of the openness of the frontiers of any particular group: and the minister's position as the normal celebrant of the sacraments, the great 'common signs' of the life of discipleship, reinforces this sense of the ministry as focusing the Church's catholicity. The minister is the custodian of the Church's memory, as a teacher and interpreter; and this will involve a reminding of the present Church that its past is flawed and calls for penitence. The minister also interprets the local community to the wider fellowship: he or she will remind a congregation that they, and their styles of life and thought, are not the centre or the norm of the Church at large, but will also testify in the wider Church to the particular story and the particular gift of the local group. And finally, there are circumstances in which the minister's job is, as a prophet of the catholic task of the church, to identify areas where gifts are being withheld, both inside and outside the visible community—to begin the work of expanding the frontiers so as to encourage a particular ministry within the lay congregation, or to open doors into some area where the service of the congregation as a whole is needed.[17] To 'guard the deposit' of the Church's confession (2 Tim. 1:14) is not to build up defensive walls around the faith; because the 'deposit' is the gospel of the resurrection, with its commission to share forgiveness with the whole world, the priest as guardian has the task of keeping the community faithful to the catholic mission.

We have already mentioned the Church's role in *judgement*; and perhaps we can here recall that the invitation to the presence of Jesus is also an invitation to penitent self-knowledge. Priest and people alike are entrusted with the memory of the world's victims, and are charged with the duty of naming them before the world. The Church is rooted in the experience of witnessing God's identification with the oppressed; it strives to show in its own life a pattern of the refusal of oppressive relations. So, in the human world, the Church is by its nature committed to the cause of the victim, which God has made his own. It must be the voice of the voiceless, dead or living. Its voice is that of George Bell, speaking (at no small cost) for the victims of saturation bombing in Germany; and that of Bonhoeffer, speaking for the Jews—'shouting' for the Jews, as he put it.[18] It may be the voice of a commemorative ceremony for the dead of Hiroshima and Nagasaki. To the objection that this simply produces an unprofitable and unrealistic guilt over actions that are now irreparable and may have been justifiable, the Church can only reply that it never seeks to generate guilt as an end in itself; but that its recollection of the fact of violence is a call to responsible acknowledgement and to conversion. Whatever may have been the heavy constraints which led men or nations to destructive acts, nothing can alter or soften the suffering caused. The Church speaks for that; yet by saying that this suffering belongs with the passion of the Saviour, the passion of God, it shows that penitent self-knowledge coincides with the knowledge of a forgiving and re-creating Lord. And it must manifest this in the fact that its judgement—like that of Jesus—is at the same time an invitation, into a new form of life and a new pattern of relation: the penitent are summoned to sit and eat at the Saviour's table, and to be themselves carriers of the gospel's judgement and the gospel's hope.

Johann-Baptist Metz, in a celebrated paper on the 'memory of suffering', has said that the Church's guardianship of this memory acts subversively in that it challenges any and every form of political domination to justify itself in the face of the past and present human cost which it involves.[19] This is well said; yet it still, curiously, suggests a clearly-defined Church calling a clearly-defined world to penitence. I believe that we have to take a further step, linking the memory of suffering with the very quality of the Church's human and relational life, and with the sacramental embodiment of this; so that the challenge is also an offer, and a *manifestation*, of new life. Metz writes: 'The memory of suffering . . . brings a new moral imagination into political life, a new vision of others' suffering which should mature into a generous, uncalculating partisanship on behalf of the weak and unrepresented.'[20] But this new vision is given to the political realm in the existence of a community of gift in which 'weak' and 'strong' are learning to cherish and respect each other, and to live forgivingly. Without a credible corporate life based on the 'memory of suffering', the moral imagination remains unfertilized. And the credibility of that life involves its *availability* to all: repent, believe, *and* be baptized.

It must be said, of course, that this complete sharing of baptismal and eucharistic life does not happen rapidly or easily, and the problem remains of how the Church is to show its openness without simply abandoning its explicit commitment to the one focal interpretative story of Jesus. To share eucharistic communion with someone unbaptized, or committed to another story or system, is odd—not because the sacrament is 'profaned', or because grace cannot be given to those outside the household, but because the symbolic integrity of the Eucharist depends upon its being celebrated by those who both commit themselves to the paradigm of Jesus' death and resurrection and acknowledge that their violence is violence offered to Jesus. All their betrayals are to be understood as betrayals of him; and through that understanding comes forgiveness and hope. Those who do not so understand themselves and their sin or their loss will not make the same identification of their victims with Jesus, nor will they necessarily understand their hope or their vocation in relation to him and his community. Their participation is thus anomalous: it is hard to see the meaning of what is being done.

Yet a request to share the Church's worshipping life with no more than a vague awareness of the significance of its symbols is not uncommon, and not simply to be rejected. It may be part of the Church's task in some places to develop what have been clumsily dubbed 'para-liturgies'—corporate symbolic actions which do not so deeply presuppose the kind of symbolic identification involved in the Eucharist, yet still open up some of the resource of Christian imagination to the uncommitted.[21] Such experimentation is another facet of catholicity and of mission—of the credibility of the Church's invitation. Far from reflecting a doctrinal indifferentism, it speaks of a very serious assimilation by the Church into the patterns of its life of the resurrection gospel: it is a way of showing itself to be essentially and fundamentally the Church of *Jesus*.

3

This conception of the Church as the voice of the voiceless leads us to some final reflections on the Spirit in the Church as the one who gives the power of *utterance*. To speak for the victim, for the forgotten and killed, requires not only the Spirit's truthfulness, to give us the awareness of this 'memory of suffering', but also an opening of our mouths: boldness to speak, to venture into the uncomfortable world of assertion and counter-assertion, debate, accusation and defence. Identification with the suffering is not only a matter of inner sympathy, nor is it only a matter of action. It means also the hard work of intelligent interpretation of the needs of the 'voiceless'. Preaching is more than mere verbalizing; but it cannot do without language, and undermines its own authority if it arrogantly refuses the ordinary speech of humanity, whether by developing a pseudo-mystical, abstract and technical idiom, or by retreating into a 'prophetic' key of pure assertion ('political' theology is all too liable to do this). Charismatic utterance, as Paul makes clear in 1 Cor. 12, is more than tongues of ectasy: it may equally be the language of education and of organized planning.

The Spirit opens our mouths for the dumb, in prophetic declamation *and* in patient and undramatic educative work. If we are to make a convincing job of naming the helpless and oppressed, we have much observation and analysis to do: if the Spirit gives utterance to us, it may be by freeing us from the paralysis induced by the complexity of a situation, so that we can risk a statement—knowing we invite denial, refutation or dismissal. The last thing a Christian should be eager to do is to minimize the moral unclarity and situational nuances of human relations; but the capacity to make articulate (even if, inevitably, provisional) judgement must not be stifled. We must allow ourselves to be given a language for this judgement by our trust in the faithfulness of the Spirit we invoke: we speak and act in the conviction that the Spirit can and will act creatively through our responsible decision—whether or not it is objectively 'right' or adequate. The Spirit may work in debate at least as much as in consensus, and we shall have done something if we have only initiated such a debate.

So in the Spirit, in the hope of grace, we are enabled to give voice to our judgement and discrimination, to name and identify both victim and oppressor. Our responsibility is two-fold: not to speak glibly or hastily, pressed by doctrinaire, or merely fashionable, influences; yet not to refuse the gift of speech when we believe ourselves to have discerned the ident-ity of the victim. Here is one practical respect in which the Spirit's gift of speech may be seen. However, the Spirit as the one who bestows the power of *naming* acts far more generally and pervasively in the life of the Church. It is by the Spirit, says Paul (1 Cor. 12:3), that we name Jesus as 'Lord'. The Lordship of Jesus is not deduced but encountered, in God's recreative agency as it makes the transaction involved in Jesus' death and resurrection limitlessly available; the com-munity of Jesus' friends is driven to enlarge and open itself, and this impulse is interpreted as God working as 'Spirit'. The fact of this 'catholic' impulse manifests the endless re-sourcefulness of Jesus' story, its universal significance; and so in the Church, by the Spirit, Jesus is found to be 'Lord', and the titles of supreme honour are given him. The Spirit enables Jesus to be named for what he is—in the life of the first small communities, in the liturgy, in the long and bitter doctrinal struggles of the early Church, in the protest of the monastic order, in the radical 'refusals' of Luther and the Reformation, in the costly *askesis* of the contemplative, and the simple gift of the martyr. In all these, Jesus is confessed, in word, symbol and act, as of unsurpassable meaning and inexhaustible re-source: as Lord.

And that act of naming and confession carries with it an-other, equally far-reaching. The Spirit is given so that we may name God as 'Father'; more exactly, as 'Abba', as *Jesus*' father (Rom. 8:15; Gal. 4:6). Because of Jesus and the Spirit, and the new human community that grows out of the resurrection, the focus of our worship, trust and comprehensive allegiance is not simply 'God', a transcendent, invisible, almighty force, but 'Father'. And that word 'Father', is not given us as a description of God (informing us that he is the source of our existence) but as an address *to* God, as the sign of a present relation, a continuing dependence. Further, the nature of that relation and that dependence is fleshed out in the life of Jesus, whose dependence on the one he calls 'Abba' is the root of his liberty and his authority. When we have been given, in the life of the community, the right to call God what Jesus called him, we have begun to find and know our God, our source and end, as the one who makes free, who nurtures us and accepts us so as to share his creative liberty with us. In the resurrection community, the fellowship of the Spirit, the creative and sustaining power of God is shown to be identical with the compassion and forgiveness that renews and reconstitutes the relations of human beings with each other. 'God' appears in human history under the name of 'the one whom Jesus calls Abba'.

Thus, if we see the Spirit's work in these terms of name-giving, it is possible to understand something of what is meant by speaking of the Church as a community where (as in the Deuteronomic tradition in the Old Testament) God chooses to 'set his name'. The community of the Spirit is the place where the context and meaning of the human world is identified concretely as Jesus with his Father and his Spirit. It is not (as we have already insisted) that there is no meaningful life beyond the community; but here it is named, and in becoming identifiable becomes more readily communicable. Christian faith and the life of the Church offer humanity a language in which to speak of its ground and its aspiration. 'There is no other *name* under heaven given among men by which we must be saved' (Acts 4:12). Christian believers make the bold claim that no other language than that which speaks of the crucified and his resurrection can speak comprehensively of what it is to be 'saved', to be whole as a human being before God. The Christian can respond to the work of human salvage and restoration wherever it occurs by 'naming' it as Christ's work. This is not to attempt any 'kidnapping' of human projects on behalf of the Church, any effort at squeezing them into the institutional boundaries of the community. It is not even to underwrite any theory of 'anonymous Christianity' beyond the Church's frontiers. But the claim *is* made that human salvage and restoration is most fully understood and becomes most fully and critically self-aware when explicitly brought to the light of the Easter proclamation of Jesus of Nazareth. Other stories and other confessions enrich the Christian's commitment: a prolonged sharing with a Jew, a Marxist, or a Buddhist will uncover facets of the human world which conventional Christian speech seems unaware of. The challenge then becomes that discussed earlier in this chapter, to manifest that such insights are essentially 'at home' with the vision of Christ as universal *logos*. If he can be found at the heart of another truthful, visionary and compassionate human project, the Easter gospel can indeed be seen to be catholic. And the pressure towards such a discovery is the pressure which keeps the Church open and imaginative: the presence of the Spirit of the risen Jesus.

Where there is salvation, its name is Jesus; its grammar is the cross and the resurrection. The Spirit which names Jesus as Lord and God as Father names the world as Christ's Kingdom, and the humanization of mankind as Christ's salvation. The resurrection of Jesus, in being a restoration of the world's wholeness, is equally a restoration of language; what is created in the community of the resurrection is not only a vision of humanity before God and with God, but a vision capable of being articulated in word and image, communicated, debated and extended. In this sense the resurrection is indeed a 'rebirth of images': beyond the dissolution of vision, the sense of loss, of guilt or alienation from oneself, there is grace given to return to language. 'Job dared to beget more sons and daughters. . . . The return to language requires an act of faith; and an acceptance of the probability of failure. It is, as such, an exercise in radical humility and an expression of the hope of "grace", communication surviving the perils of words.'[22] We go back, therefore, into a messy and compromised realm, to words that will never properly bear the meaning laid on them ('Father' is a colossally problematic word, as we are so often reminded),[23] yet confident that it is within this 'family' of symbols flowing from *ta peri Iesou tou Nazarenou* that the ultimate, definitive (absolute, if you like) truth about the human world and its context takes intelligible, communicable form; that our stammering and groping among these massive, resilient words and images is somehow 'Spirit-breathed'.

And one, very paradoxical, ground of this trust lies in the fact which Christian contemplatives constantly bring before us, the fact that Christian speech is *for ever* entering into and re-emerging from inarticulacy. There is not one moment of dumbness or loss followed by fluency, but an unending flow back and forth between speech and silence; and if at each stage the silence and the loss and emptiness become deeper and more painful, so at each stage the recovered language is both more spare and more richly charged. Those who make facile criticisms of the non-falsifiability of religious language might well consider this aspect of it—its negative and self-critical response to its own constructs and models. When Christian speech is healthy, it does not allow itself an over-familiarity with, a taking for granted of its images—its Scriptures, its art, its liturgy; it is prepared to draw back to allow them to be 'strange', questioning and questionable. And if we return once more to the classical narratives of the resurrection, we shall find some intriguing material for reflection in this regard. The alternation of the familiar and the strange is one of the most haunting features of these stories: reading them not only as a text about experiences but as a text about religious language itself, it is possible to grasp some significant points about the genesis of a distinctively Christian mode of theological language—distinctive in both method or style and content. So in the next chapter, we shall try to see how the theme of the familiar stranger, the alien friend, takes shape in the gospel stories and how it shows something of the whole process which brought Christian theology as such into being as a new mode of talking about God.

Notes

1. See G. W. H. Lampe, *God as Spirit* (OUP 1977), pp. 50–3, and chapter 2, *passim*, for a careful and sensitive discussion of the differences between Old Testament models of the Spirit's activity as (more primitively) transitory rapture or possession and (in the canonical prophets and the Wisdom literature) as the heightening of natural capacities in relation with the divine.
2. Michael Harper, *Bishop's Move* (Hodder & Stoughton 1978), pp. 29–30.
3. Herbert McCabe, O.P., *Law, Love and Language* (Sheed & Ward 1968), p. 33.
4. A famous example was the Cold Comfort Farm project of Guy and Molly Clutton-Brock in Rhodesia; see their delightful and courageous *Cold Comfort Confronted*, (London, Mowbrays, 1972).
5. For an account of the development and character of the L'Arche communities see Bill Clarke, S.J., *Enough Room for Joy* (DLT 1974). Vanier himself expounds his understanding of the task of L'Arche in *Community and Growth* (DLT 1980).
6. On the practice of excommunication in the early Church, see most recently Ladislas Orsy, S.J., *The Evolving Church and the Sacrament of Penance* (Denville, New Jersey, Dimension Books 1978), pp. 31–4. On the theological questions involved, cf. Karl Rahner, 'Forgotten Truths Concerning the Sacrament of Penance', in *Theological Investigations* II (DLT 1963).
7. This holds true even in overtly non-sacramental Christian communities: the corporate silence of the Society of Friends certainly has the character of an 'identifying' action, redirecting the community to its source, even though that source is not here seen in straightforward 'event' terms.
8. See, e.g. Paul Evdokimov, *L'art de l'icône. Théologie de la beauté* (Paris and Bruges, Desclée de Brouwer, 1970), pp. 245–6; note the connection made here with the Orthodox rite of the 'blessing of the waters' at Epiphany, which is above all a celebration of Christ's *baptism* in the Eastern tradition.
9. See C. K. Barrett, *The Gospel According to St John*, pp. 190–2, for a convenient summary of the problems associated with this passage.
10. See the excellent remarks of Vladimir Lossky, *In the Image and Likeness of God* (New York, St Vladimir's Seminary Press, 1974), p. 118.
11. *Essays on Biblical Interpretation*, ed. with an introd. by Lewis S. Mudge (SPCK 1981), p. 144.
12. So that Paul's phrase in Gal. 1:16 about the revelation of God's Son *in* him, Paul, is applicable to the life of the whole Church. For a human life to receive God's grace is a 'showing' of God *in* that life, an event of manifestation to the world.

13. Lossky, op. cit., p. 221 (in the course of a seminal and profound discussion of power, human and divine).
14. Cf. Rowan Williams, 'Poetic and Religious Imagination', *Theology* (May 1978), p. 182, on the distinction between language as the communication of ideas from someone who has them to someone who does not have them, and language as the construction of shared human possibilities.
15. From an address on 'Catholicity and Mission to the World', *St. Vladimir's Theological Quarterly* (1973), vol. 17, nos. 1–2 (containing papers given at the Second International Conference of Orthodox Theology in 1972, on the theme of 'The Catholicity of the Church'), pp. 107–8.
16. The now classical exposition of this is John Zizioulas' essay, 'The Eucharistic Community and the Catholicity of the Church', in John Meyendorff and Joseph McLelland, ed., *The New Man. An Orthodox and Reformed Dialogue*, (New York, Agora Books, 1973). See also, for some of the sources of this approach, Lossky, op. cit., chs. 8 to 10.
17. See Patrick J. O'Mahony, *The Fantasy of Human Rights* (Great Wakering, Mayhew-McCrimmon, 1978), for an account of how one congregation was aroused to a genuinely 'catholic' involvement in the worldwide struggle for justice and compassion.
18. Eberhard Bethge, *Dietrich Bonhoeffer. Theologian, Christian, Contemporary* (Collins 1970), pp. 360–1.
19. Metz, *Faith in History and Society*, p. 115.
20. Ibid., pp. 117–18.
21. See the remarks of Lakshman Wickremesinghe, Bishop of Kurunagala, Sri Lanka, in *Today's Church and Today's World* (preparatory articles for the 1978 Lambeth Conference) (Church Information Office 1977 and 1978), p. 81. I must acknowledge a great debt in the whole of this chapter to conversations with Bishop Wickremesinghe.
22. Williams, 'Poetic and Religious Imagination', p. 182.
23. See the *Concilium* symposium, *God as Father?* ed. J. -B. Metz and Edward Schillebeeckx (Edinburgh, T. & T. Clark, 1981), especially the essays by Dominique Stein, Dorothee Soelle and Catharina Halkes.

CHAPTER FOUR

Talking to a Stranger

1

The Christ who travels towards Jerusalem and suffers there can be made into a familiar. The risen Christ is something suddenly unknown. This metamorphosis had always in the past represented for Barney simply a disappointment, like the ending of a play. He had never thought of it as a starting point. He thought of it so now for the first time; and, with this shift of view, it became clear to him, with a sudden authoritative clarity, that it was the risen Christ and not the suffering Christ who must be his saviour: the absent Christ hidden in God, and not that all too recognizable victim. He was too horribly, too intimately connected with his own degraded image of the Christ of Good Friday. Easter must purge that imagery now. The scourged tormented flesh appealed to something in him that was too grossly human since he had not the gift of compassion. These sufferings ended for him in self-pity and further on and shamefully in pleasure. This could not alter him a jot though he contemplated it forever. What was required of him was something which lay quite outside the deeply worked pattern of suffering, the plain possibility of change without drama and even without punishment. Perhaps after

76

all that was the message of Easter. Absence not pain would be the rite of his salvation.[1]

Iris Murdoch here depicts, with all her usual acuteness, a decisive moment in the process of liberation from self. The chaotic Barney, with his sexual inadequacies, his academic failure, his pathetically self-justifying private journal, discovers that his absorbing and complex self, and the little dramas which he writes and produces for it, is not after all the focus of the world; he must learn emptiness, non-interference, action with no attempt at control, the loss of a cheaply dramatic model of his life. 'He must not expect [his wife] to help him to make a tidy drama out of his infidelities or to make him suffer in exactly the way he wanted.'[2] And this transformation, this conversion, is a shift of perspective from the cross to the empty tomb—Barney's experience occurs, indeed, in the course of the Easter Mass. It is a transition from the destructively familiar to the creatively strange.

Christ crucified too readily becomes simply the God of my condition. There is no problem about 'identifying' with Jesus on Calvary if our own world is one of failure and humiliation; and if we believe Jesus to be God incarnate, we may be consoled at the thought of God sharing our suffering. Yet Luther more than once criticized those who 'mingled' their sufferings with Christ's: those, presumably, who saw their own sufferings, self-inflicted or not, as giving them some kind of guaranteed share in Christ's grace by assimilating their state to his. Dorothee Soelle has in turn criticized Luther for thus implying that human suffering is incapable of sharing in the significance of Christ's cross, and so reducing present pain or misfortune to something morally and theologically neutral.[3] I think, however, that she has missed the point of Luther's strictures, and so missed a vitally important and problematic dimension of 'devotion to the crucified'. It is precisely when Christ's sufferings and mine are brought intimately together that the image of the crucified is indeed in danger of degradation. We experience ourselves as sufferers, as victims, and so experience Christ's cross as the symbol of who and what we are. Jesus as victim is the image of myself as victim. God, making himself a victim in the death of Jesus, affirms *me* in my suffering: he is (in Whitehead's celebrated phrase) the 'fellow-sufferer who understands'.

Now it is of course essential that there should be a way of giving significance to what I suffer, and Dorothee Soelle is entirely right to protest at any theology or ideology which strips anyone's suffering of significance and commends a merely passive endurance. To use the cross of Jesus as a vehicle for making sense of my suffering, a symbolic mediation which gives my experience back to me newly located and interpreted, is not necessarily an illegitimate step to take. But symbolic mediation is a slippery matter: if my interpretation simply stops at this point, I risk turning the cross itself into a defence of my position, a legitimation. This is how the cross can be made to serve an ideological purpose. God is identified with *my* cause, because he is identified with *my* suffering: the cross is the banner of my ego—or the banner of a collective ego. If I suffer I am in the right, because God 'endorses' my pain.

We saw in the first chapter how important it is to distinguish God's identification with the victim from some kind of divine moral approval of the victim's cause; and, in the last chapter, we discussed that misunderstanding of martyrdom which distorts it into a defensive argument for a particular case. If the cross is used primarily or exclusively as a symbol of my suffering, it is being used as a weapon against others in a way exactly parallel to (and closely connected with) this defensive use of the martyr's memory. *I* am crucified, *you* are the crucifier; I am victim, you are oppressor; I am innocent, you are guilty. The path leads alarmingly on to the statement, 'My suffering is deeper, more significant than yours'; and thence to, 'Nothing I inflict upon you is of comparable significance to what you have inflicted upon me.' It is the peculiar blackmailing logic of terrorism, from the direct psychological 'terrorism' of diseased family relationships to the indiscriminate and anarchic violence of kidnap and hijack.

In this dark region of human interaction, suffering becomes an immensely desirable, invincible weapon, because it is a guarantor of justice and of innocence. The high risk and the practical futility of a fair number of terrorist enterprises amount to an invitation to more suffering: there is little hint of a search for transformed relations. And in the Christian context, there is unmistakably present in some styles of Christian spirituality a commendation of suffering and humiliation precisely along these lines. Suffer in order to be innocent; make the cross *your* cross, and you will be armed with righteousness, in the assurance that God is with you. And, as Iris Murdoch's Barney reflects, this kind of reception of the cross as symbol alters nothing and seeks to alter nothing; the symbol becomes little more than a somewhat magnifying mirror for my condition—and a mirror also for my self-approval, my defining of a secure and righteous position over against the other. Self-pity, leading into the pleasure of knowing the impregnable moral armour of innocence: this is indeed how the cross can be made the ego's servant. If this is what Luther condemned, he was right to do so.

The cross ceases to be an ideological weapon when it is recognized not only as mine but as a *stranger's*; and it is the stranger (as Barney recognizes) whom we meet on Easter morning. To stop with Good Friday is to see the crucified simply as reflecting back to me my own condition, and even to remember the crucified, in the superficial sense, can merely leave us with a martyr for our cause. The women come on Easter morning to look for the corpse of a martyr, and they find a void. If we come in search of the 'God of our condition' at Easter, we shall not find him. 'You seek Jesus of Nazareth who was crucified . . . . he is not here' (Mark 16:6; cf. Matt. 28:5–6). Holy Week may invite us to a certain identification with the crucified, Easter firmly takes away the familiar 'fellow-sufferer'. It does not even allow him to be a consoling memory, a past hero; he is not here because he is risen, because his life continues and is not to be sealed off with a 'martyr's' death.[4] There is at Easter *no* Christ who simply seals our righteousness and innocence, no guarantor of our status, and so no ideological cross. Jesus is alive, he is there to be *encountered* again, and so his personal identity remains; which means that his cross is his, not ours, part of the history of a person who obstinately stands over against us and will not be painlessly assimilated into our own memories. We have seen already how the Easter Jesus is both judge and restorer because he can say to us, 'I, and not you, am the crucified.' And I have tried to show that our restoration is contingent upon hearing these words and acknowledging our responsibility as crucifiers. We have to begin by seeing the cross as the cross of our victim, not of ourselves as victims. It is true that the wheel will come full circle, and we shall be enabled to find part of our identity in terms of privation and diminution; but this can only happen in a fully transforming, 'saving' manner if it is bound up with the discovery of the whole human world (not just me) as characterized by privation—the discovery, in fact, of that *compassion* which Barney lacks, a passionate engagement in suffering which is not one's own.

To be given the picture of myself as crucifier, as I am given it in the Easter encounter, is to make an important discovery about the nature of suffering itself. Pain is not simply what I endure, it is equally what I transmit. To concentrate upon the cross as *my* cross locates the responsibility for pain elsewhere—with God, with nature or fate, with those who have the power I do not. To see the cross as another's is to learn that pain and violence is something I am capable of causing. If the responsibility for suffering is always elsewhere, the fact of suffering may seem automatic and inevitable. Even if it is inflicted by other human beings, they form a *class* of powerful and violent people different from myself as sufferer, fixed in their action and attitude by my separation from them. But when I find myself responsible for the diminution of others, I discover what David Jenkins has called a 'solidarity in sin',[5] which is, paradoxically, hopeful. If I am involved in the transmission of violence, I cannot pretend that violence is something I can do absolutely nothing about; and if I discover, through this recognition, a possibility of transformed relationship with the other in whose suffering I have colluded, this makes some difference to the structure of the violent world. I am, willy-nilly, involved in 'structural violence', in economic, political, religious and private systems of relationship which diminish other (and I must repeat once more that the victim in one system is liable to be the oppressor in another: the polarity runs through each individual). Yet I find, through the resurrection gospel, that I have a choice about colluding with these systems, a possibility of belonging to another 'system' in which gift rather than diminution is constitutive. I am thus equipped to understand that structural violence is not an unshakeable monolith: critical action, constructive protest, is possible. My involvement in violence is most destructive when least self-aware, and simply understanding that involvement is a crucial first step. But to understand it in the presence of the Easter Jesus is to understand that violence is not omnipotent, and that my involvement in it does not rule out the possibility of transformation of my relations. What human beings make they can in some measure re-make or reform (not un-make). I grasp that I am a maker of oppression; but also that this is not all I can make, given the ground of creative forgiveness. Of course, the pattern of destructiveness in our world is inherited by us, not invented by every new generation (it is continually extended and elaborated precisely because it is inherited, because we *begin* 'diminished', as we saw in chapter one), and so it cannot be wholly reconstructed by any one generation. Yet the critical presence of a new humanity in Jesus witnesses to the fact that the world is not a prison in which we must accept the inevitability of all pain because it is beyond our responsibility. To know ourselves as crucifiers is to know ourselves as responsible: we are able to say yes or no to violence, to accept or to protest.

So Easter does carry with it the possibility of change, in the individual and in humanity; but that possibility depends upon understanding the cross first of all as 'not mine'. So far from resting content in an easy assimilation of my suffering to that of Jesus, I have to allow myself first to be parted from the 'fellow-sufferer' and see my suffering in the perspective of the pain of a whole world where neither I nor anyone else except the crucified God is a pure victim. I must meet the crucified Jesus again as a risen stranger, who will not allow me to define the world in terms of undifferentiated and unalterable pain, but insists that suffering is produced by the complex interrelation of persons, by the impulse to reject self and others. The Jesus who returns on Easter morning establishes firmly and inescapably the polarity between oppressor and victim as a fundamental datum of our world; there is a gulf to be bridged, a wound that will not be healed until we have seen that it is bleeding.

He is not here. 'What you thought you came for/Is only a shell, a husk of meaning.'[6] Easter means coming to the memory of Jesus, looking for consolation, and finding a memory that hurts and judges, that sets a distance, even an alienation between me and my hope, my Saviour. Easter occurs, again and again, in this opening-up of a void, the sense of absence which questions our egocentric aspirations and our longing for 'tidy drama'; it occurs when we find in Jesus not a dead friend but a living stranger. Some modern writers have—carelessly?—spoken of Jesus being raised 'as' the believing community, or alleged that the risenness of Jesus consists essentially in the persistence of Jesus' own faith and trust in God within the Church. Yet this sidesteps the whole issue of the strangeness of the risen Jesus. He is never permitted to be assimilated into the 'martyr for our cause': it is impossible to recover in the New Testament any layer of belief or interpretation which sees Jesus as a martyr and no more. We have already noted that Jesus as risen is a Jesus who cannot be contained in the limits of a past human life; the corollary of this is that Jesus as risen cannot be contained in the legitimating and supporting memory of a community. The Church is not 'founded' by Jesus of Nazareth as an institution to preserve the recollection of his deeds and words; it is the community of those who meet him as risen and the place where all the world may meet him as risen.

'We had hoped that he was the one to redeem Israel', says Cleopas (Luke 24:21). The memory of a man who had given flesh to the hope of Israel's redemption would be worth treasuring, even if this hope had never been fully realized, had indeed been violently cut off. But the elegiac, the wistful retrospect of the tragic hero, is not to be the key in which Jesus' disciples speak of him: Cleopas is not the definitive theological voice of the first believers. Cleopas *possesses* a mem-

ory of Jesus; yet he is aware (vv. 22–4) of the disturbing and
disorienting absence of a corpse, a tangible memorial; and he
addresses his remarks to a questioning stranger. The empty
tomb at least prevents him closing off his story as an elegiac
memory; but it remains problematic—'him they did not see'
(v. 24). It still remains for him to lose that conventional
martyr's tale as he recognizes the stranger for who he is. He,
and the other disciples, *will* 'see'. In Cleopas' little speech,
Luke takes us into the very middle of that reconstruction and
redirection of understanding that is the Easter experience, the
process in which we are forcibly parted from the consoling
recollection assimilated with ourselves and confronted with
one who is still and forever *other*.

One of the strangest features of the resurrection narratives
is precisely this theme of the otherness, the unrecognizability,
of the risen Jesus. Three major stories (Luke's Emmaus episode, John's account of Mary Magdalene at the tomb, and
the 'Galilean fantasia' which concludes his Gospel) underline
the point. Whatever the experiences of the disciples at Easter
were, it is hard to deny that this element must have played
a part—that for some at least, the encounter with the risen
Jesus began as an encounter with a stranger. And this is one
of the most important pieces of evidence counting against the
suggestion that the risen Christ is to be seen as a projection
of the community's own belief, its sense of continuity with the
identity of Jesus. In the Emmaus story, Jesus sharply rebukes
Cleopas for his failure not only to grasp the foreordained
character of Messiah's sufferings but to make the connection
between suffering and 'glory', between the cross and creative
freedom and power. Jesus condemns the inadequacy of their
earlier understanding: he is not what they have thought him
to be, and thus they must 'learn' him afresh, as from the
beginning. Once again, John crystallizes this most powerfully
by presenting the disciples in their fishingboats, as if they had
never known Jesus: they must begin again.

So the void of the tomb and the unrecognizable face of the
risen Lord both speak of the challenge of Easter to a God who
is primarily 'the God of our condition'. The Lordship of Jesus
is not constructed from a recollection but experienced in the

encounter with one who evades our surface desires and surface needs, and will not subserve the requirements of our private dramas. The Church is not the assembly of the disciples as a 'continuation' of Jesus, but the continuing group of those engaged in dialogue with Jesus, those compelled to renew again and again their confrontation with a person who judges and calls and recreates. The Church may be Christ's 'Body', the place of his presence; but it is entered precisely by the ritual encounter with his death and resurrection, by the 'turning around' which stops us struggling to interpret *his* story in the light of *ours* and presses us to interpret ourselves in the light of the Easter event. The 'Body' image is one of many. We need to be cautious about any tendency to see the Church as a simple 'undialectical' extension of Christ; and we have already explored something of the way in which the Eucharist enshrines the dialectic by *both* confronting us with our victim *and* identifying us with him. The Church is where Christ is because it is where persons find their identity through him and before him. Christ is with the believer and beyond the believer at the same time: we are in Christ and yet face to face with him. Christian worship and spirituality wrestles continuously with what this means, as it both addresses Christ directly, *and* speaks in his name to God as 'Abba'.[8] Jesus grants us a solid identity, yet refuses us the power to 'seal' or finalize it, and obliges us to realize that this identity only exists in an endless responsiveness to new encounters with him in the world of unredeemed relationships; to absolutize it, imagining that we have finished the making of ourselves, that we have done with desire and restlessness, is to slip back into that unredeemed world; to turn from the void of the tomb to the drama of a cheapened Calvary for the frustrated ego.

2

The notion that faith involves a purification of desire is deeply embedded not only in Christianity but in other religious traditions: its radical expression in concrete forms of life is monastic asceticism; in personal spirituality, it is the *via negativa*, the stripping of self by detachment from palpable experiential 'rewards' in prayer. What I have been arguing in this chapter so far is that the resurrection can and should operate as a central symbol for the purification of desire and the de-centring of the ego, because the necessary first moment in the resurrection event is one of absence and loss. I am not, after all, provided with the equipment to console myself, but instead am summoned to a revaluation and re-location of myself, and a reinterpretation of my desire. 'What you thought you came for/ Is only a shell'; and what you thought you wanted is disallowed, shown to be egocentric fantasy. Back to Iris Murdoch's Barney at the Easter Mass: what I want is revealed as the continuance of a situation in which my ego supposes itself to be in control. And this wanting, while superficially a longing for a new and more congenial situation in which I can rest, is in fact a barrier to actual change. The root fact that I am not 'at home' in myself and my world stirs me to desire; but if that desire is a wanting to be *in possession* of self and world, a wanting not to lose the ego's imagined pivotal position, it can only intensify my sense of dis-ease. I have to learn another kind of desire. Authentic desire for change is a desire which puts into question what I now am, recognizing incompletion, poverty; and so it also puts into question what I *think* I want. If I acknowledge lack, I acknowledge an inability to prescribe exactly what will supply that lack. There is a fundamental level at which I have to say, almost nonsensically, that I do not and cannot know what I want.

That is the level where alertness and receptivity must begin. If we acknowledge our poverty, the next step is to open our eyes and wait for the manifestation of a truth that will transform and liberate. The stripping away of the longing for 'tidy drama', a shapely narrative of which I am the hero, is the precondition of hearing ourselves called and finding ourselves situated in a new world. The freedom or the absolution for which I seek will be created as I learn to respond to this calling and to the limits of my situation as newly shown to me. And the Christian gospel describes this calling as the address to me of my risen victim, who shows me how my egotism is itself a sign of lack and poverty, by which I inflict lack and poverty on others. Jesus communicates to me the truth that I am accepted and forgiven 'absolutely'—i.e. by the eternal God—so that there is no need for my ego to compensate for its privation by the depriving of others. The want to dominate and diminish is rooted in ignorance of God as Father. When that illusory want is done away with, my desire is set free: I am entitled to *want*, to care about, the healing and fulfilment of the whole of my human world. My desire is translated into compassion—or, reverting to the categories of the previous chapter, my own response to grace becomes inseparable from the mission to share it.

At each stage, I seek finality; my illusory wants return. Hence the phenomenon we discussed at the end of the last chapter, the 'unending flow back and forth between speech and silence', and hence the importance of the resurrection for our grasp of the nature of religious language. We have a language for Calvary, all too familiar a language: we are used to talking about suffering, ours and the world's, and we are tempted to rest content with speaking of a suffering God, whose infinite sympathy somehow makes the world's pain bearable or intelligible. The empty tomb silences us: the memory, the *monument*, of the Great Fellow-Sufferer vanishes. There is, it seems, more to be said; yet it is by no means clear what can be said. We rightly shrink from a hasty response to Easter morning which blandly says that Jesus, our God-in-Jesus, has triumphed over pain and death, has done with it, so that what seemed tragic is really not so. 'The absent Christ, hidden in God' may appear simply to witness to an ultimate separation between God and suffering. The empty tomb, then, is indeed a moment of inarticulacy, doubt, and even (as for the women of Mark 16) fear, of disorientation and the sense of abandonment ('They have taken away my Lord. . . .').

And when the risen Jesus appears, to give us back our speech, when the sense of meaningfulness and affirmation seizes us again, we are not asked to describe or systematize. The language given us is that of self-knowledge, penitence, and that of preaching and absolution: it is the language of *confession*, in the double sense of that word so richly exploited by Augustine. This is a language which maintains the possibility of stripping and questioning, and which lays bare to the world how this may be a process of self-recovery, and the creation of renewed relations. A language which stayed at Calvary would resolve the problem of suffering passively; while the language of Easter is inextricably bound up with the practice of the Church, in prayer and mission alike. In one way, it leaves Calvary a greater problem than ever, but it also affirms that it is not a problem whose resolution is in words—even words about the suffering of a compassionate God.

Calvary becomes more problematic because, when the risen Christ is finally recognized, it is of course *as* the crucified. So far from pain and death being bypassed or 'transcended' in the usual sense, they are presented to us as now interwoven with God as we encounter him. The question of my salvation and my significance revolves around the figure of the risen and exalted Lord, the ultimate focus of all human meaning; and that exalted Lord is one who has endured rejection and murder. So the question of my 'salvation and significance' becomes a question about my response to the fact of pain generated by violence. To discover, to grow into, a reconciled identity for myself, I must go by way of this response. And to find the crucified one exalted as Lord is to know that the problem of suffering is never going to leave us alone: it cannot be caught and sealed and buried, even by the response of passive acceptance. In the resurrection, it is presented as the 'unconditional', the universal question. I shall not be asked at the last day whether I have 'suffered well', I shall be asked how far I have allowed Christ's questioning to transform my life into compassion, and how far, therefore, I have allowed compassion in me to transform the world. All of which is a laboured way of restating the parable of the Great Assize in Matt. 25, or the accusatory 'Why are you persecuting me?' of Jesus to Paul. The king's question is one about compassion, and thus about the purification of desire. The risen Christ who hides and eludes and appears-and-vanishes is the sufferer *as other*, who cannot be trapped in the coils of my unreconstructed desire, which pulls the world in towards myself. To respond to the sufferer as other is to move away from the drama of *my* pain, to be drawn by the world, not to draw it; and this is compassion, the transformation of desire for which distance, absence and strangeness are necessary conditions.[9]

Understood thus, the resurrection becomes the moment which overthrows an idolatrous view of grace, idolatrous because it sees grace as serving *my* needs as I define them. The Reformation reacted with perhaps unbalanced savagery against a spirituality of imitation and of identification with the crucified, and the indiscriminateness of this response was to impoverish the Protestant ethos for some time. But this reaction is an essential part of the Reformers' struggle to enthrone grace in its proper freedom and majesty, and to shatter the comfortable fantasy of a grace which warms, affirms and rewards without ever nurturing growth by question and judgement. At this level, the Reformation—with many aspects of the Counter-Reformation, for that matter—represents a crucial move towards adulthood in the history of Christian understanding: *not* by any means that all that went before was infantile, but that here is an articulate and decisive rejection of certain pervasive kinds of infantilism—fantasies of gratification, undifferentiated dependence, the effort to please (and thus 'harness') a parental authority. Every proper proclamation of the Easter gospel, pointing to a hidden and elusive Christ with whom we can never simply and unconditionally identify, represents the same challenge, the same rejection, the same call to 'adulthood'. The resurrection calls forward into a life that is genuinely new and effectively changed by a grace which both displaces the ego from its central and domineering position and grounds the self more and more profoundly in the accepting love of the Father.

Thus the risen Christ can say both, 'Do not hold me' (or 'Do not touch me') to Magdalene, and 'Put your finger here and see my hands; and put out your hand, and place it in my side' to Thomas (John 20:17 and 27). The risen Jesus *is* ascending, in John's rich phrase, he is receding from our grasp and we are not to struggle and cling; yet when he is seen, the exalted Lord is recognized, made particular, given

content, by the fact that he bears tangible human scars, and
forever confronts us wounded. The familiarity of his pain is
not simply the familiarity of our own; it is the all too recognizable face of the world whose suffering we have helped to
make, and which we cannot therefore draw into ourselves.
Grace deals with us whole: it does not simply console me as
victim, for that would be to leave untouched the reality of my
complicity in the hurt and damage of the world. Human
beings long to be reassured that they are innocent. But this
is one of the cardinal points of misdirected desire, a desire to
possess or to manipulate a power capable of obliterating part
of ourselves and our past. The gospel will not ever tell us we
are innocent, but it will tell us we are loved; and in asking us
to receive and consent to that love, it asks us to identify with,
and make our own, love's comprehensive vision of all we are
and have been. That is the transformation of desire as it
affects our attitude to our own selves—to accept what we
have been, so that all of it can be transformed. It is a more
authentic desire because more comprehensive, turning away
from the illusory attraction of an innocence that cannot be
recovered unless the world is unmade. Grace will remake but
not undo. There is all the difference in the world between
Christ uncrucified and Christ risen:[10] they speak of two different kinds of hope for humanity, one unrealizable, the other
barely imaginable but at least truthful.

3

In effect, what we have been considering in this chapter is a
further dimension of the *freedom* of the risen Christ. We have
already spoken of how the resurrection frees Jesus from the
boundaries of the merely local in time and space; and we may
now see also how the resurrection frees Jesus from our projections and expectations. 'We had hoped that he was the one
to redeem Israel': we were not wholly wrong, but the unfamiliar risen Lord will show us how little we know of the
meaning of 'redemption' or of 'Israel'. 'Not less of love but
expanding / Of love beyond desire',[11] beyond the immediately

graspable limits of a self-focused desiring. And here we may pause to think of the implications of this language about Jesus' freedom. He is, we have said, free from local limitation, and free from the limitation of belonging to the past: without ceasing to be a particular person in a particular place, he is capable of interpreting an unlimited range of human situations. He is 'catholic', as his Church aims to be, he is for all, and there is no place or time or condition to which he is alien, or where his story and his Spirit have nothing to give. And if this is so, there is no place or time or condition in which he can be domesticated, in which we can say that his story and his Spirit are exhaustively defined. He is utterly unsusceptible to definition; and while we may continue to burden him with our hopes, fantasies and projections, there is an obstinate and restless dimension of unclarity which will break through and challenge sooner or later. He is constantly 'not here'. He is always the partner as well as the self-image, the stranger on the shore, in the garden, on the road, eluding identification and control. As such, he stands as a stark reminder that it is only in confronting the partner and the stranger that we meet him. He compels us to a self-forgetful 'attention' to all strangers and all dialogue partners—those of other races and cultures, of other faiths, of other Christian confessions, those with whom we have to work co-operatively, those with whom we create our 'private' lives, in marriage, family or community. To let the other be strange and yet not reject him or her, to give and to be given attentive, contemplative regard—this is all part of our encounter with a risen Lord.

Yet at the same time, it is the encounter with this stranger which generates our own most central sense of identity, of 'being at home', so that the believer can invite the whole human world to find a home in the same encounter. He is not to be found in us, but we hope to 'be found' in him (Phil. 3:9). Our ultimate place in the order of things is with or in the risen Jesus. And this also means that our ultimate place is not alone, but with all those others who have found their home in him—a potentially limitless company—because we find this place precisely through our reconciliation with others by means of Christ's forgiveness. Salvation is never for me alone, but for me and those who have been my victims and those who have been my oppressors. Around that magnetic centre of the person of Jesus risen and exalted there is room for us all, since through the medium of this figure the complex multiple relationships which bind people in mutually destructive patterns can become relations of gift and mutual enrichment. Because his resurrection embodies the paradigm of merciful reconciliation, it enables men and women to be at home with themselves and with one another as well as with God. It is in this way that the resurrection gospel speaks of the last things, of a completion of history in the purpose of God: the resurrection community shows humanity in its ultimate reality. It speaks the truth about our present condition, but it also speaks the truth about humanity as God wills it to be: it manifests the primary and irreducible *meaning* of what it is to be human, the fundamental context of human existence, as the purpose of a compassionate creative will, a will for love.

In these ways, what we say about Jesus begins to take on more and more clearly the tone and character of what we say about God. Jesus is not to be tied down to any set of worldly configurations and constraints, although he is never a merely abstract term. He eludes and questions our predictions and projections, recedes and hides before our attempts to arrive at adequate, definitive statements. And he embodies for us a creative purpose, a basic meaningfulness, of comprehensive scope—a statement of how the world *is* in God's will, and therefore of what it can and should be. Positively, then, Jesus as the central and comprehensive resource of meaning in the world has the same role in our thinking and striving as does God. Negatively, his elusive, enigmatic quality, always probing and unsettling, works in our language as does the confession of God's 'transcendence'. A theology of the risen Jesus will always be, to a greater or lesser degree, a *negative* theology, obliged to confess its conceptual and imaginative poverty— as is any theology which takes seriously the truth that God is not a determinate object in the world.

The risen Jesus is strange and yet deeply familiar, a question to what we have known, loved and desired, and yet continuous with the friend we have known and loved. His strangeness and his recognizability are both shocking, standing as they do in such inseparable connection. And so with God: to call him 'Father' is to acknowledge not only closeness and familiarity, but rootedness in his will, and yet 'Father' must be addressed to him from the depths of experiences of lostness, darkness and alienation (as it was by Jesus in Gethsemane). The risen Jesus returns as a loved friend and brother, and at the same time holds us off: he shows the marks of familiar human pain, yet refuses to be only a consoling mirror-image of our suffering. He holds us off and yet welcomes us to break bread with him, to renew a fellowship broken by our infidelity. He will not be either friend or foe as we understand those words; and it is in not being controllable by our wishes and fantasies that he appears akin to God, a true son of the Father who is both unimaginably close and unimaginably strange. The dialectic of the resurrection stories is the dialectic of all our worship and contemplation, so that to see in the risen Jesus both an endlessly receding horizon and a call to journey more and more deeply towards our centre and our home is to see him as God-like: more simply, to see him as *God*, because he is the concrete form in which we encounter this infinity of challenge and infinity of acceptance most clearly and comprehensively. The project of a limitless expansion of the heart which we understand as the call addressed to us from beyond the limits of everyday understanding, from outside 'the world', the hope of a transformed future in which human relations will be fully what they can and should be, all this is manifest to us in and *as* the crucified and raised Jesus.

Christian prayer thus operates all the time between almost contradictory poles. It begins with Jesus and it sets itself in the context of Jesus: in his name and his place, it calls God 'Father', and looks constantly to the record of how he lived out his sonship, even to the point of death and hell. Yet it encourages a deep and fierce suspicion of words, images, particular kinds of experience, and insists on the need to press on in darkness and formlessness, in an absence of obvious meaning (let alone of gratification). When this is spoken of abstractly, when we read Origen, Cassian or Meister Eckhart exhorting us to abandon meditation on the humanity of Jesus, which belongs to an 'elementary' stage of spiritual life, it can sound sub-Christian, anti-incarnational, élitist, mystificatory, what you will. Yet it is undeniable that we do have to reckon with an historical life that itself urges us away from its historical limits, that opens on to immense horizons: a life that does not end but is somehow drastically altered after Good Friday. Meditation on Jesus should never forget that Jesus is risen; yet the character of the exalted, hidden Lord who leads us on in darkness, and the nature of the human destiny to which he calls are given shape and intelligibility only because he is also the crucified Jesus of Nazareth.

Easter is indeed a 'purgation of imagery', as Iris Murdoch suggests, yet never simply a rejection of images; as we have seen, it gives us speech as well as reducing us to silence. But it is, so to speak, a narrative account of the programmatic point which theologians have repeatedly made about the inescapable tension between affirmation and negation in their language. Jesus, in short, is shown to have in common with 'God', as the word is normally used, the characteristics of focusing our sense of creative purpose (he defines our 'last end'), of sketching the limits of what it is to be human before God, and of eluding any exhaustive or systematic account of his significance. He *gives* meaning, and does not need to receive it from elsewhere; the only source of interpretation for his life before and after Calvary is 'the Father', the one to whom he prays. Yet that Father is not a definable agent over against him: it is he, Jesus, who in word and deed, gives content to the word 'Father'; the Father is not shown in the world in acts of power but only in Jesus. It is not that Jesus appeals for his authority to a clearly-defined heavenly being, whose will and nature can be plainly described; he receives the shape and direction of his life as a call from one whom he knows uniquely and authoritatively, so that his life itself becomes the word, the communication, which gives form in the eyes of others to the unknown 'Father'. 'No one knows the Son except the Father, and no one knows the Father except the Son and any one to whom the Son chooses to reveal him'

(Matt. 11:27). 'God' and 'Jesus' are unintelligible abstracted from each other. Thus the Easter Jesus can be said to have been raised *by* the Father (as in Rom. 8:11 and 1 Cor. 15:15 and other passages): what Jesus is still derives from no source other than 'the Father', the one to whom he prays. And now, after Easter, the reciprocity between Father and Son is plainer than ever: *all* the Father's authority belongs to Jesus (Matt. 28:18), Jesus goes to the Father, to take his throne beside him. More than ever, Jesus is 'unknown', unintelligible without the Father, without the sense that his new being is grounded in the life of the creator; more than ever, the Father is unknown without Jesus, without the form given to his creativity by the process of renewal and reconciliation initiated by the risen Jesus.

Two unknown poles, only intelligible in their mutuality: prayer and theology alike occur in the interplay between these poles, impelled and directed by the authoritative prompting which shows them to be necessary to each other, shows that the movement between the poles is essential to the life of redeemed men and women. 'Father' and 'Son' interpret each other in the motion of that unnameable third term we call 'Spirit'. The exalted Jesus' belonging with the Father leads ultimately into that supreme Christian affirmation of the divine elusiveness, the divine 'mobility' and life—the doctrine of the Trinity.

The New Testament writers, of course, do not arrive at any such formulation. But it remains true that for them the resurrection and exaltation of Jesus are in process of creating a new language for speaking of God. Jesus' post-resurrection status means that there is nothing *between* Jesus and his Father: no mediatorial powers intervene to block or limit his relation to the Father. He is exalted above all angels, he is in some sense prior to or superior to the mediated revelation of the Torah (here Paul and the writer to the Hebrews are in profound concord). The God of Israel habitually deals with his people through mediating powers (so the Jews of the period held), but the whole of this system is irrelevant to Jesus; and to those who come to be 'in' Jesus, it is equally irrelevant. No power can intervene between Christ and God, and this means too that 'neither death, nor life, nor angels, nor principalities, nor things present, nor things to come, nor powers, nor height, nor depth, nor anything else in all creation, will be able to separate us from the love of God in Christ Jesus our Lord' (Rom. 8:38–9). Christians must learn to speak of a God from whom their lives are not to be separated, a God, therefore, involved with the whole fabric of their being— a God who accepts and justifies and adopts. And because of this powerful sense of an interweaving between the divine life and our own, Christians will take up the Hellenistic language of 'sharing the divine nature' (as they do already in 2 Pet. 1:4) and give to it a new colouring, a Christological basis, which will make it pivotal in the theology of the first Christian centuries. From this also comes the profound early Christian sense of life as testimony (and *death* as testimony), communicating and witnessing to the good news of God's act in Christ: life itself can speak of God, even when the words to do so run out,[12] because God has been woven into the texture of life as its controlling image and 'myth', its resource of meaning. To live the forgiven life wholeheartedly *is*, as we noted in the last chapter, to speak of God.

From the first, the risen Jesus represented for believers a place where the meaning of 'God' and the meaning of 'humanity' overlapped. Speaking of Jesus meant speaking within the range of possible meanings covered by the generic term 'human being' (even within the New Testament, we can see how the early believers resisted the strong pressure to move their language about Jesus out of this range into the area of myths about temporarily embodied spiritual individuals); yet it was also, from the perspective of the new community shaped by encounter with Jesus risen, to speak within the range covered by the word 'God'—to speak of creativity, finality, ultimate authority, inexhaustible living presence, universal significance. Creative love can belong with the conditioned state of created humanity: it is possible to be human without being trapped in a net of mutual destructiveness. All this is there to be grasped in the story of Jesus' exaltation to God's throne—an exaltation which yet does not cancel or call into question his identity as a member of the human race.

How is such a story to be told except by means of such enigmatic records as we have? 'The Lord' is and is not Jesus of Nazareth, belonging with us and beyond us. This is where the resurrection encounter generates something radically fresh in speech and narrative. The extraordinary difficulty of reducing the resurrection stories to any familiar narrative 'type' from the Jewish or Hellenistic repertoire testifies eloquently to this newness: there is no lack of cliché, convention, and allusion to familiar forms—the apotheosis of heroes, the assumption of prophets and patriarchs—yet not even one of the gospel accounts, let alone four, can be finally and satisfactorily dealt with under the heading of a single literary convention.[13] The stories are irregular and unconventional, we must assume, because whatever lay behind them was unexpected and deeply bewildering. The Synoptic evangelists take some pains to scatter predictions of passion and resurrection around in their accounts of the last period of Jesus' ministry; yet, when they come to the event itself, it is abundantly clear that they are confronted by a disorderly bundle of traditions whose sole common feature seems to be the conviction that nothing which occurred on Easter Day or after was anticipated. We read of fear, grief, doubt, ecstatic joy, but not of a simple sense of prophecy fulfilled. Now of course the 'amazement' of the disciples is as much a literary convention as the 'amazement' of the crowds who witness Jesus' miracles. Yet it is hard to dismiss the consistent echo of disorientation and surprise. The curious romantic reductionism which speaks of 'hysteria behind locked doors' generating hallucinations simply ignores the oddity and pluriformity of the traditions as we have them. A chronicle of Easter Day would be a hopeless enterprise, and the conflict of traditions has still to be satisfactorily sorted out.[14] The retellings of the story by both conservatives and radicals have so often been bland and facile. Perhaps all we can recover across the centuries is the piercing note of shock; and that says a great deal.

Even in the Gospels, one thing is never described. There is a central silence, not broken until the second century,[15] about the *event* of resurrection. Even Matthew, with his elaborate mythological scenery, leaves us with the strange impres-

sion that the stone is rolled away from a tomb that is already
empty. Jesus is not released by an angel (like Luke's Peter,
in Acts 12), but raised by the Father. It is an event which is
not describable, because it is precisely there that there occurs
the transfiguring expansion of Jesus' humanity which is the
heart of the resurrection encounters. It is an event on the
frontier of any possible language, because it is the moment in
which our speech is both left behind and opened to new
possibilities. It is as indescribable as the process of imaginative fusion which produces any metaphor; and the evangelists
withdraw, as well they might. Jesus' life is historical, describable; the encounters with Jesus risen are historical and (after
a fashion) describable, with whatever ambiguities and un-
clarities. But there is a sense in which the *raising* of Jesus, the
hinge between these two histories, the act which brings the
latter out of the former, does not and cannot belong to history:
it is not *an* event, with a before and after, occupying a determinate bit of time between Friday and Sunday.[16] God's act
in uniting Jesus' life with his eludes us: we can speak of it
only as the necessary condition for our living as we live. And
as a divine act it cannot be tied to place and time in any
simple way. It is, indeed, an 'eternal' act: it is an aspect of
the eternal will by which God determines how he shall be,
his will to be the Father of the Son. These are abstract words,
they describe nothing. They can only point to the truth that
God's being and will are always and necessarily *prior* to ours.
The event of resurrection, then, cannot but be hidden in
God's eternal act, his eternal 'being himself'; however early
we run to the tomb, God has been there ahead of us. Once
again, he decisively evades our grasp, our definition and our
projection.

> I got me flowers to straw thy way;
> I got me boughs off many a tree:
> But thou wast up by break of day,
> And brought'st thy sweets along with thee.[17]

Notes

1. Iris Murdoch, *The Red and the Green* (Chatto & Windus 1965, Penguin Books 1967), p. 230.
2. Ibid., p. 231.
3. Dorothee Soelle, *Suffering* (DLT 1976), pp. 130–1.
4. See Gerald O'Collins, s. J., *The Calvary Christ* (SCM 1977), especially chs. 1 and 2, for a powerful exposition of the impossibility of treating Jesus under the conventional category of 'martyr'.
5. David Jenkins, *The Contradiction of Christianity* (SCM 1976), ch. 5, especially pp. 67–73.
6. Eliot, *Little Gidding*, I, lines 31–2.
7. See, e.g., James Mackey, *Jesus, the Man and the Myth* (SCM 1979), pp. 117–20, 259, 261–2.
8. Even in the New Testament, Jesus is addressed and petitioned as 'Lord'—almost certainly in 1 Cor. 16:22 (a pre-Pauline, probably liturgical, formula), in Rev. 22:20, and in Acts 7:59—although the ultimate focus of devotion is still Jesus' God, the Father.
9. Compassion as the fruit of a purgation—or even cessation—of desire is of course the central and distinctive concept of Mahayana Buddhism, with its ideal of the compassionate *bodhisattva*, who denies himself bliss in order to enlighten others; see, e.g., John Bowker's account in *Problems of Suffering in Religions of the World* (CUP 1970), pp. 259–68.
10. A difference fatally blurred for instance in Edwin Muir's celebrated poem, 'The Transfiguration':
    'Then he will come, Christ the uncrucified,
    Christ the discrucified, his death undone,
    His agony unmade, his cross dismantled
        . . . . and the betrayal
    be quite undone and never more be done'
    (*Collected Poems*, Faber, 1960, p. 200).
11. *Little Gidding* III, lines 157–8.
12. Cf. Rowan Williams, *The Wound of Knowledge* (DLT 1979), pp. 18–19, on the significance of silence in Ignatius of Antioch's understanding of testimony and revelation, both in Jesus and in the Church.
13. As an illustration of this difficulty, see Schillebeeckx, *Jesus. An Experiment in Christology*, pp. 340–4, where the author attempts (with evidence from the work of G. Lohfink) to assimilate the Lucan narratives to a 'rapture' or 'assumption' stereotype in the Hellenistic and Jewish *milieux* of the day. It must be said that much of the argument is forced in the extreme: apart from the dating of some of the evidence, which is either questionable or rather too late, the crucial point of a correspondence in vocabulary is not established.
14. We have already touched, for instance, on the Galilee–Jerusalem problem and the debateable background of Paul's catalogue in 1 Cor. 15.

On the latter, see Hans Conzelmann's commentary on 1 Cor. (Philadelphia, Fortress Press, 1975), pp. 256–9, and C. K. Barrett's commentary (A. & C. Black 1968 and 1971), pp. 341–4.

15. When the Gospel of Peter provides a highly-coloured description of the exit of the glorified Christ from the sepulchre: E. Hennecke—W. Schneemelcher, *New Testament Apocrypha*, vol. I (Lutterworth 1963), p. 186.

16. See the very suggestive, though brief, discussion in R. H. Fuller, *The Formation of the Resurrection Narratives* (SPCK 1971), p. 181.

17. George Herbert, *Easter*.

CHAPTER FIVE

The Risen Body

1

We come finally to reflect on that aspect of the resurrection narratives about which the keenest and bitterest debates have raged in this century. The risen Jesus is by no means, for any of the New Testament writers, a resuscitated body and no more; yet he relates to his disciples in recognizably bodily ways. He speaks and is heard; it is possible to touch him; he eats (in Luke 24:41–3, he apparently does so precisely to make the point that he is not a 'spirit'). In fact, he relates to his disciples as he has done before. The resurrection stories of Luke and John at least are not stories of theophanies or visions in the Old Testament tradition. They belong in the same world as the narratives of the ministry. It is *because* of this ordinariness that the strangeness discussed in the last chapter can emerge in such sharp relief. Seeing the exalted Jesus, the Jesus who belongs with God, is disturbingly like meeting any human being—disturbingly, because the shift of perspective which recognition and confession involve is that much more drastic. Once more, it is a matter of categories being blurred: to meet an exalted, apotheosized human being in a vision like that described in the first chapter of the Apocalypse makes some kind of sense; but to meet him on a road or around a table is far more bewildering.[1] Some such considerations must have shaped the unwillingness of so many

100

New Testament writers simply to treat the resurrection as 'cancelling' the crucifixion, *replacing* humiliation with 'glory'; and at the end of this particular line of development stands the fourth evangelist, for whom 'glorification' comprises cross and exaltation in indissoluble connection. The risen Jesus is 'going up' to the Father, yet without simply sloughing off the human condition.

Meeting the risen Jesus, then, both is and is not a special kind of experience. It poses uniquely acute problems of description, yet it is apparently not an experience which involves any extraordinary means of knowing or seeing. 'Vision' is a clumsy category for such events, since its normal usage carries overtones of the private, the limited and the exceptional. Jesus appears only to a few, and yet his presence with the disciples and his availability to all is, as we have seen, strongly insisted upon. 'I am risen and I am *with* you' is the message of the Easter Jesus. The apparitions are not fleeting manifestations of a normally absent being, but events which establish Jesus' *presence*, the interweaving of his life with the life of his community. The risen Jesus in the gnostic gospels of the early Christian era is the Saviour, who having secured his own liberation from the corrupt world, returns in glorified, discarnate shape to give to his apostles detailed instructions for their own escape.[2] His apparitions are indeed private and exceptional visitations whose purpose is to give saving information; whereas the New Testament apparitions—if our reading of them in this book so far is correct—aim both to restore and to enlarge a relationship of gift and trust among human beings, which is itself God's gift, through Jesus, to the whole human world.

The relation of Jesus risen to his disciples is continuous with the relationship they have already known: it is not suddenly privatized, turned into an obscure reverential memory. In his ministry, Jesus created and sustained the community of his friends by speech and touch and the sharing of food; and so, after his resurrection, that community is maintained in the same way. It is not taken away from history, from matter, from bodies and words.

That the usual representations of resurrection have given rise to misunderstanding, there can be no question of doubting; but that the schema of resurrection itself should be charged with 'materialism' seems to us to be the result of a nonsensical assumption. In fact, what this schema aims to safeguard is not the earthly form of life we now experience, but the link between man, the world and the other which gives structure to this form of life. The biblical schema of resurrection imposes nothing beyond this affirmation: God by his power brings human existence into a new relation with the 'cosmos' and with others, a relation of such a kind that the previous form of existence is not negated but exalted.[3]

To be close to Jesus, in material relation with Jesus, during his ministry was to be close to the *embodied* love of God, God's final and total forgiveness made concrete in the flesh of a man, his words and his acts. Again, we return to the point touched on in the first chapter: grace is not abstract. The good news of the resurrection involves the affirmation that grace does not become abstract with the event of Jesus' physical death.

This means, at least, that the resurrection faith is inseparable from the existence of an historical human community characterized by certain styles of relation, such as we have already sketched.[4] This is the dividing line between the New Testament accounts of resurrection and—on the one hand—gnostic fantasies of esoteric instruction by a discarnate Redeemer, and—on the other—an antiquarian interest in the fate of a particular human corpse.[5] 'At least': this is the minimum we need to say in order to ensure some sort of continuity between the New Testament proclamation and our own theologizing about Easter. It is not to say that this precisely encapsulates or exhaustively describes the 'real' content of the resurrection stories. We cannot quite so easily remove or ignore the element of conviction about an identifiable material presence of Jesus in the immediate post-Easter period. Yet of course the Church continued to exist when there were no more 'apparitions'; and we are encouraged to believe that the faith of a later generation of Christians in the risen Christ is not different in *kind* from the faith of the apostles on Easter Day. John (20:29) certainly implies that a faith which can promptly detach itself from any need for apparitions is more mature than a faith which needs to 'see'. And this text is quoted with almost wearisome frequency by those concerned to minimize the material and tangible aspects of Jesus' risenness.

But what Thomas is being invited to believe in—and we in turn, without the tangible assurance given him—is still *the risenness of the crucified Jesus*, and his renewed material contact with his friends. Thomas' failure is not in misunderstanding the nature of resurrection but in demanding a special, individual assurance of it: he wants a proof other than the testimony of the group of believers. Beyond the first, irrecoverable moment of encounter, it is essentially through the Church that the world comes to belief, not by an indefinite series of 'special' events: such seems to be John's point, a point entirely in accord with the themes of the Farewell Discourses of 14–17 (see especially 17:20–3). A resurrection appearance designed to prove the reality of Jesus' risenness, divorced from the establishing of the community's faith, can only be, at best, anomalous. If such a concession is granted to Thomas, it is presumably, in John's eyes, to complete the manifestation to the *whole* apostolic band, to re-establish the whole community of Jesus' friends. It would be a nonsense for anyone else to ask or expect it.

The resurrection faith is bound up with the existence of the community, then; but that does not immediately answer the question of the source of both faith and community. Taken overall, our evidence suggests that it is not at all clear when the apparitions ceased, and that it does not especially matter. Luke produces his tidy scheme of forty days culminating in an ascension or assumption; John's Gospel in its present form offers three apparitions, the last being completely undateable; Paul believes that the last apparition was his own encounter on the Damascus road, yet grants that there was something untypical about it (though whether in 1 Cor. 15:8–9 he means that it is irregular because late, or irregular because it is a showing to someone with no previous contact or fellowship with Jesus is entirely obscure). However, it also suggests that no one thought in terms of a faith generated independently of some sort of primal encounter, and an encounter of a specific and concrete kind. That is to say: there is something *prior* to the community. In chapters 3 and 4, I have attempted to sort out a little the senses in which it is and is not true to see the Church as 'identified' with the risen Jesus: the Church is where Jesus is met, where bodily, historical grace and reconciliation are now shown, it is the 'body' of Jesus' presence; but the Church still meets Jesus as an other, a stranger, it never absorbs him into itself so that he ceases to be its lover and its judge. The Church may be the body, the fleshly reality, in which Jesus' grace is apprehended. But what was the 'body' in which the first believers apprehended it?

This is not a rhetorical or a loaded question; there are several intelligible answers. Perhaps the simplest is to say that this 'body' was indeed the apostolic group itself in the process of its re-formation. As the apostles discovered, gradually and painfully, that it was possible for them to belong together once again, possible to forgive themselves and receive forgiveness at each others' hands, and 'own' together their memory of betraying their Lord and betraying each other in desertion and flight, the tangible formation of acceptance and restoration was to reconstruct for them the kind of fellowship they had known with Jesus. In their learning of mutual grace-giving they learned that their relation with Jesus was not severed, and interpreted their corporate forgiveness as his act, his 'return' to them.

This, I think, would provide a good account of the process of deepening understanding out of which a theology—or rather several theologies—of resurrection and exaltation began to develop. It is not fanciful to assume that the conviction of the risen Christ as gracious judge could only take root in a community that had understood in its own life what grace meant. The apparition on the Damascus road alone would not have given Paul *faith* in the risen Jesus—we might say—isolated from his subsequent experience, chequered as it was, with the fellowship of believers. But to use that example leads

us straight back to the problem we have been trying to cir-
cumvent. Can we say anything of an event initiating the
process? Even to speak of Peter's 'conversion' as the corner-
stone of the resurrection faith, as it is now common to do[6]
(despite the lack of any specific account of this in the New
Testament), does not absolve us from the challenge of this
question. To reduce the basis of the Easter gospel to a single,
private experience on the part of Peter is unduly to simplify
the confusion and pluriformity of the primitive witness. And
I am not sure that this helps to account for that echo of
bewilderment, shock and disorientation which we have noted
in our stories. The risen one, the exalted one, addresses the
community from *outside*. The horizon of the apostolic band is
forcibly opened up by a manifestation which takes a very long
time to understand and 'unpack'. So the Gospels and Paul
imply.

And for all four Gospels, the story which identifies the
ultimate source of this disorientation is that of the empty
tomb. This, at least, provides a clear basis for what is on any
other showing very hard to explain, the primitive confession
that Jesus was raised 'on the third day': the process of ap-
propriating the Easter gospel has a definite, even dateable,
beginning. It is *just* possible that this is a purely conventional
index of the passage of time, that it refers back to Hosea 6:2
('After two days he will revive us; on the third day he will
raise us up, that we may live before him'). But this ignores
one important piece of evidence: that the Christians seem,
from very early on, to have celebrated the resurrection on the
day after the Sabbath, 'the Lord's day'. The references in the
empty tomb narratives to 'the first day of the week' likewise
suggest (being obviously a traditional item in the story) that
'the third day' meant exactly what it said. There is a definable
beginning to the process of resurrection encounter, and it is
the discovery of the absence of Jesus' corpse.

The story as it stands also provides a very clear ground for
the primitive sense of the resurrection gospel as a message
from outside. The grave is discovered by people outside the
apostolic band itself, and it is these 'marginal' figures who
are charged to go and preach to the community: 'Go, tell his

disciples and Peter . . .' (Mark 16:7).[7] The very first thing
that generates a hope and wonderment about the possibility
of encountering Jesus afresh is the message from an outsider,
a *woman* (not only socially marginal for the Eleven but also,
of course, one whose evidence could not be adduced in the
customary procedures of Jewish law—so that her testimony
cannot be assimilated into familiar legal structures), that his
body is not to be seen. In almost every respect, this is em-
phatically a 'strange' message; yet it is one which has a simple
basis in verifiable fact (Luke and John suggest that some of
the disciples did indeed take the trouble to verify it). The
empty tomb certainly does not create resurrection faith, but
what it does do is to guarantee that when the community
encounters the mercy and the calling of the risen Lord, it
interprets his risenness in a certain way. The Jesus who
comes to the disciples is a Jesus concretely continuous with
the earthly leader and friend of the days of the ministry. If
his body is not in the tomb, then that must be what is met
when Jesus is met—hence the Lucan and Johannine stories
designed to emphasize that the apparitions have a material,
objective pole. Matthew at least is perfectly well aware that
the tomb story is not a sufficient condition for resurrection
faith; but that is not to say that the evangelists are mistaken
in seeing it as a *necessary* condition.

Let us try to recapitulate a little. The Easter faith is seen
in the New Testament as a response to a specific call, which
takes time to assimilate and understand. And if this is so, it
is hard to reduce its basis to a single visionary experience, or
even to the community's own developing experience of corporate grace. Something must have provided a first stimulus,
and, more importantly, a structure of presuppositions within
which subsequent experiences could be organized. The empty
tomb tradition proposes just such a stimulus and structure:
the apostles are drawn together by receiving the message that
Jesus' body is not in its grave, and this helps them to understand what later happens as an encounter with a Jesus who
is, now as hitherto, a partner in dialogue, a material other,
still involved in the fabric of human living while also sover-
eignly free from its constraints. This leaves a good deal of

latitude in dealing with the apparition stories: it certainly points us away from any simple view of individual or corporate 'self-authenticating' visions, and allows fully for their enigmatic and elusive nature. As matters stand, we have no apparition stories that do not bear the mark of extremely sophisticated literary editing: all we possess by way of early testimony is the list reproduced by Paul in 1 Cor. 15. We can have little clarity as to what the 'seeing' of Jesus here described actually involved.[8] We can only assume that it made some kind of sense in the early community to speak of it in terms of meeting an identifiable person, recognizing a face. The location and timing of the apparitions is equally obscure; and ultimately we come back to our familiar point, that the whole sequence of happenings is only really visible and intelligible in and through the community and the particular quality of its life. But we do well never to forget that the object and ground of the community's faith is not its own life, but that to which its life is an answer:the 'word from beyond', the message from the tomb.

2

The positive point in all this is, let me repeat, that the resurrection does not absolve the believing community from taking history seriously.[9] If Jesus' ministry had communicated to the apostles the possibility of human flesh carrying divine meaning, God being 'enacted' in the acts of a man,[10] the resurrection seals this discovery, vindicates and completes it. The marriage of heaven and earth is consummated in the risen Jesus, not ended. But notice: we speak of Jesus' *acts* as bearing divine weight. If we say that Jesus in his ministry 'embodies' the grace of God, we do not and cannot mean that the grace of God is identifiable with Jesus' material and biological constitution. We are, rather, asserting that grace takes tangible form in what Jesus (as a material being) says and does in the world of material beings. If we are to say of Jesus that he is God's 'body' in the world, we must at once make it clear that we mean the life, the history, of Jesus, what he makes, the relations he sets up. It is absurd to think here of 'body' and 'embodiment' referring simply to Jesus' physicality, although this is the necessary identifying centre for speaking of his acts and effects. Put in another way, it is not simply Jesus' bare presence that is 'gracious', but Jesus present—as he most characteristically is—in words and deeds that make grace concrete, that *create* healing, forgiveness and fellowship.

Thus Jesus' characteristic hospitality extended to the rejected and marginal, and his acceptance of their hospitality extended to him (see, e.g., Mark 2:15ff, and parallels) is a paradigm instance of 'embodied' grace. In word and act, Jesus rejects the world's rejections, and causes the rejected to become accepted. In his sharing of food with the tax-collectors and sinners, he creates for them a new relation with each other and with God by bringing them into relation with himself. The means by which God is met is a transaction which perceptibly changes the prevailing human state of affairs so that the victims become guests, receivers of gifts. Thus the shared table is the natural and indispensable extension of the 'embodiment' of grace in Jesus' person: embodiment takes effect in the acts of the person.

It takes effect decisively, of course, in Jesus' acceptance of his approaching death, and in his enduring of it: this is where he becomes visibly and actually the embodying of a love that opposes violence, and where Jesus demonstrates conclusively his response to a vocation of self-gift. So, on the eve of the passion, Jesus performs an act which fuses together the hospitality and acceptance of his ministry and the radical self-offering he is to accomplish on Calvary. He takes food and drink and says that his sharing of them with the Twelve is grounded in the deeper act of self-sharing which is nearing its consummation: what he gives is himself, all that he shares with others belongs in the context of self-gift, takes its meaning from that context. 'This is my body.' The breaking and sharing of bread *signify*, have weight and resource, because they belong to the breaking and sharing of Jesus' selfhood. So the grace which is 'embodied' in the events of Good Friday is 'embodied' likewise in this act. Jesus' hospitality changes the status of men and women, brings them into the world of gift; and that it does so depends upon Jesus' entire identity being gift, even to the point of death. Calvary is the cost of his hospitality, Calvary most radically and finally changes the status of the lost and the guilty: so there is one focal act of 'hospitality' where the symbolic connection is made. We are invited to grasp the truth that to eat at Jesus' table is to benefit from his total self-offering—in historical terms, from his death on the cross. Our redemption, our transformation, experienced as we find ourselves his guests, depends on nothing less.

Hence the enormous importance of the stories of the risen Jesus breaking bread with the disciples. By their desertion, their complicity in his murder, they have ranged themselves with the lost and the guilty, they have made themselves 'marginal' to the reality of God's Kingdom. What they have to learn is that, if Jesus is indeed *wholly* given over to living and dying as 'gift', nothing but their own hardness of heart and lack of trust can disqualify them from receiving the grace he has to give. Thus, to welcome or be welcomed by him at a meal on the further side of Calvary is the ultimate assurance of mercy and acceptance, of indestructible love. And the meal of the Christian community becomes the fullest available embodiment and effective sign of the grace of the crucified for the whole world. Since it is *after* Calvary that it assumes its richest significance, the community's meal with Jesus is invariably an 'Easter' event (and so most properly celebrated on the first day of the week). The Eucharist, as the meal which presents to us the reality of Jesus' giving and recreating activity, is never a commemoration of Maundy Thursday alone, nor merely an extension of an ordinary 'fellowship meal' of Jesus with his friends (however meaningful such meals were), nor even a re-presentation of Calvary *tout simple*: it enacts for us the risenness of the crucified as the inexhaustible gift of mercy among us, in our common life. Almost all Christian traditions (with the possible exception of the Eastern churches) have at times in their history settled for celebrating the Eucharist as if Easter had nothing to do with it, as if, indeed, Easter had never happened. And if it is so celebrated, it is hardly surprising if men and women fail to see it as a focal identifying symbol of the life of the resurrection community.

To take food as from the hand of Jesus after Easter is to receive from him the gift of his essential being—that presence of truth and acceptance before which we find again our lost selves. His food is the bread of life, 'and the bread which I shall give for the life of the world is my flesh' (John 6:51): to eat Jesus' food is to recognize the gift of himself behind it, and so to eat his flesh. And John continues by having Jesus say: 'Unless you eat the flesh of the Son of man and drink his blood, you have no life in you' (6:53). Without the material presence of Jesus in the meal which his community shares, restoration and enrichment do not occur; if Jesus is not encountered in this concrete form, his work is not done. Granted that (as has been said above) there are many styles of community in which reconciliation may be met, many places where the bread of life is offered un-named, two things remain true: that this bread is 'food indeed' (John 6:55), human and material love; and that the Church's Eucharist is the uniquely full articulation and bringing to light of Jesus' restoring grace in an authentic manner only when it is the meal of a community that actively seeks to live in reconciliation. This is not to enter into the rather sterile debate as to whether a Eucharist celebrated in a deeply and impenitently divided community is or is not 'valid'. Paul, in 1 Cor. 11:27–30, alarmingly suggests that if Christ's presence is invited by such a community, he will not refuse; but the dishonesty, the untruth and unfaith of the community means that he can be present only as judge, with deeply destructive effects. There are circumstances in which the Eucharist cannot be rightly celebrated, and to learn to recognize such circumstances can be an important step in maturation: it represents a growth in truthfulness—and so, paradoxically, a receiving of at least one aspect of the gift which the Eucharist embodies.[11]

There is a further point to be drawn out here. If in his acts of hospitality, especially in the culminating hospitality of Maundy Thursday, Jesus 'lends' to material objects, food and drink, the significance of his own personal will and being, makes them part of his self-gift, it is made clear to us that the grace he gives is not restricted to his flesh and bones. As we have already said, the shared table is an 'extension' of embodied grace. We might go on from here to say that Jesus can in some measure 'inhabit' the material world beyond the limits of his biological existence: his life is communicable through what is not biologically his body, because his activity of breaking bread is so tightly bound to what he is, to the manner of life he lives. During his ministry, this communicability of his life, his significant being, is limited by the limitations of his biological existence: it occurs, necessarily, only in the place where he happens to be, with the people he happens to be with. Now if we are right in seeing in the resurrection the liberation of Jesus from the constraints of ordinary human individuality, it is clear that the communicability of his significance is no longer limited in the same way. The 'life of Jesus', the presence of his grace, can inhabit what is not literally his flesh even in circumstances remote in time and space from the historical location of his flesh; and this occurs when the resurrection transaction of restoration and reconciliation is effected 'materially'.[12] If the risen Jesus is present where men and women turn to their victims and receive back their lost hearts, then he is 'materially' present where this process involves a specific material transformation—where the effective significance of material things is changed.

As has been said, the Christian Eucharist provides a central interpretative model for this: our food and drink is given up into the hands of Jesus so that we become his guests and receive our life from him. The elements are shifted from one context of meaning to another,[13] from being our possession to being gifts given and received back (and in spite of a proper caution about speaking too loosely of the elements as 'offered' to God in the Eucharist, we still need to say that the moment of *relinquishing what is ours* is crucial in the eucharistic process). But this transaction does not occur exclusively in the Eucharist—and indeed its 'occurrence' in the Eucharist in isolation from its occurrence in the Christian community's life is, as we have remarked, a gross offence against the true significance of the sacrament. It occurs whenever we make the essential transition from seeing the material world as possession to seeing it as gift: as God's gift to us, and as, potentially, a gift to be given and received between human beings.

The transformation of the world is not merely a change in attitude: if we see the world as gift, we see it as something *to be given*, as the call to give. The 'transformation of the world of persons' discussed above must always take full account of the fact that personal relations have a straightforwardly material dimension. The oppression and violence, the chains of destructiveness, which we have been reflecting upon are embodied things; they occur socially, economically, and quite simply physically. They occur in connection with the possession of the world's resources. When material reality is taken, dominated and hoarded in order to become part of the order of meaning I construct for myself (and the 'I' here is as much collective as individual), it is incapable of being inhabited by the 'significant being' of Christ, because it cannot be a symbol of mutuality. Thus it locks Christ out, and constitutes a denial of Christ's Lordship: it is a sign of unbelief in the resurrection. When convertedness is embodied in a transforming of economic relationships, material reality will have become charged with the life of Christ risen: the world will be revealed as his.

So the Eucharist, and every 'eucharistic' activity in which the meaning of the material world is transformed from possession to gift, is a sign not only of restoration and peace among human beings, but of the ultimate Lordship of the risen Jesus in which this restoration and peace is grounded. This is the sense in which the Eucharist is a sign of the end of all things, the consummation of Christ's Kingship: here is a part of the material world wholly and unequivocally given over to the significant being of Christ, embodying his culminating gift on the cross; here a part of the world is 'named' without reservation as Christ's (and we may refer back here to our earlier treatment of 'naming' as the work of the Spirit to give us some sense of the transforming role of the Spirit in the Eucharist). The Eucharist demonstrates that material reality *can* become charged with Jesus' life, and so proclaims hope for the whole world of matter.[14] The material, habitually used as a means of exclusion, of violence, can become a means of communion. Matter as hoarded or dominated or exploited speaks of the distortion and ultimate severance of relationship, and as such can only be a sign of *death* (which is, as we have seen, the ultimately isolating event for unredeemed humanity). The matter of the Eucharist, carrying the presence of the risen Jesus, can only be a sign of *life*, of triumph over the death of exclusion and isolation. The classical language which describes the Eucharist as the 'life-giving mystery', or even 'the medicine of immortality'[15] still has a profound validity.

If the Eucharist is a sign of the ultimate Lordship of Jesus, his 'freedom' to unite to himself the whole material order as a symbol of grace, it speaks also of creation itself, and the place of Jesus in creation. The French Jesuit theologian, Gustave Martelet, in a brilliant study of resurrection and Eucharist, speaks of 'a world that has been created for the Resurrection'[16] and of faith in this mystery 'revealing to us the true and ultimate identity of the world'.[17] The resurrection reverses the 'normal' order of the fallen world in which nature triumphs over meaning: the precarious balance in human life between action and passion, dominating and being dominated, is resolved at death into sheer passivity, being dominated, and the human imposition of form on the world is defeated. The resurrection shows us Christ as wholly 'dominant', unconditionally active, and so holds out the promise of a transformed human relationship with the cosmos.[18] The influence of Teilhard de Chardin upon P. Martelet's argument introduces some ambiguities for those uneasy with evolutionary mysticism and predominantly supra-personal (or impersonal) frames of reference, but the point can be stated in other terms. To say that Christ's relationship with the cosmos is dominant is to say that, because of him, the enterprise of giving meaning to the world is not defeated by death. Over and above the imperfection, the failure and the transitoriness of our attempts to live 'significantly' and to create a shared significance, a shared dignity and security, for the whole of humanity, there remains an inexhaustible source of transforming vision and power, affirming the value of these efforts and so continually reawakening hope. The 'identity' or the goal of the created order is to be discovered, not invented: the pattern of gracious acceptance, free and mutual gift, is not to be extinguished because it does not depend upon us. What Jesus is is the embodiment of creation's hidden truth: he is the *logos*, the meaning of all things, made flesh.

Thus eschatology leads us back—as it did the earliest Christian writers—to 'protology', the doctrine of the beginning of things, and Christ as Lord and Judge points us back to Christ as creative Word and Wisdom. If we make Eucharist in full awareness of what we are doing, celebrating the Lordship of the risen Jesus, we confess him as God's Word, Alpha no less than Omega. And our attempt to live eucharistically, to transform our world into a community of gift, is more than merely obedience to a command, more than the imitation of a remembered historical pattern of life: it is the uncovering of the eternal *sapientia* of God. It seeks to realize the sense, the meaningful structure, of creation, its groundedness in what God is. If it is true to say that there is creation because God is essentially self-sharing, then the fact of the world's existence—of our existence, of the existence of material things—will remain nonsensical until we recognize the primacy, in terms of meaning, of the activity of gift and sharing. This is the activity that makes sense of things, because this is the activity which shares in God's own significant being, in final and fundamental *truth*.

The Eucharist as the celebration of Jesus risen is the way in which the Church actually finds *and* proclaims in its own life the truths which these reflections have endeavoured to set out: the possibility of forgiveness, of reconciliation with the stranger, the healing of our lostness and deprivation, by means of Jesus' being set free for all the world in his resurrection; the understanding of the Church's task as the universalizing of Easter, the creation of a universal community of gift; the confession of Jesus of Nazareth as Lord and God, sharing the elusive and challenging and endlessly fertile nature of God the Father. In the Eucharist, the Church hears repeatedly the word of judgement and of grace, the heart of its identity and source of its sense of meaning, a call to transforming action. To take 'the world' in the eucharistic elements and name them as signs of Jesus, signs of creative love and reconciling gift, is to recognize the possibility of the world's transfiguration, in the name and power of Jesus, into a world of justice and peace; not to allow this possibility to be realized, not to act in such a way that our belief in transformed relations is made evident, is to be convicted of unbelief. We do not trust the risen Jesus: which means that we do not trust ourselves to be forgiven or others to be forgivable. 'If Christ has not been raised, your faith is futile and you are still in your sins', wrote Paul (1 Cor. 15:17); and if we are still in our sins, we have not yet truly heard the news that Christ has been raised.

3

This consideration of the Eucharist may well raise once again in our minds the question of the early community's experience of the risen Jesus. Earlier in this chapter, I suggested a possible account of this in which the 'body' of the risen Jesus was in fact the apostolic community itself, discovering grace in its life together. Luke, in Acts 4:32–5, describes the primitive Church very clearly in terms of a 'community of gift' centred upon the breaking of bread; and while this is obviously an idealized and homogenized picture, it does indicate how the connection between resurrection and a certain style of common life and ritual was grasped at a very early stage. It is then possible to say that the primary occasion for 'resurrection encounter' by the apostles was at the eucharistic meal?[19] even that the 'body' of the risen Jesus is simply the eucharistic assembly? In the light of some of the points made in the last section of this chapter about the possibility of Jesus' 'body' being more than his flesh and bones and his life being communicable 'in circumstances remote in time and space from the historical location of his flesh', this would seem to be an appealing proposal. Perhaps the message of the empty tomb combined very shortly after the crucifixion (on Easter Sunday evening, as Luke and John claim?) with a corporate experience as the apostles broke bread together to generate the first apparition story? If we suggest further that the message of the empty tomb actually *prompted* the Eleven to meet and break bread in memory of Jesus, the connection would be still more obvious to make; and this would be the beginning of that process of discovering grace together, in one another, an event which assured them collectively that they were not rejected by their Lord.

I confess that I find this an attractive and plausible reconstruction; and for that very reason, a dubious one. It helpfully allows for a measure of agnosticism about the actual fate of Jesus' body (the emptiness of the tomb as such proves nothing) and about the nature of the apostles' 'seeing' of Jesus: that is to say, it is congenial to a frame of mind uneasy with the miraculous, though not wishing dogmatically to exclude the supranatural. But this immediately makes it suspect as an interpretation of a first-century text or texts. It also evades the difficulties raised by Paul's list of apparitions, a catalogue that is obviously of some antiquity, in which individual and corporate 'seeings' mingle bewilderingly. We have no means of telling on the basis of this list whether there was any traditional *narrative* connection between the apparitions, whether the sequence of the list indicates a real chronology (it may already represent a combination of earlier formulae)—though Peter's position at the beginning and Paul's at the end are clearly significant. It is quite possible to conclude that some of the 'seeings' were independent of any others[20] (an early tradition about the appearance to James suggests something like this).[21] And if we do allow for the possibility of more than one apparition to an individual, we cannot simply reduce the whole tradition to the confines of a corporate interpretation of what happened when the apostles found for the first time that they were again able to remember Jesus eucharistically. It does seem that the prompting to 'celebrate the Eucharist' again after the crucifixion did *not* come only from the (deeply ambiguous) message of the empty tomb. As we have suggested, this latter provides a framework for understanding what subsequently occurred; but that later occurrence must still have been of such a nature that it was possible for an individual—Peter, James, Paul—to feel himself or herself confronted by another identifiable person. Bread is broken at the initiative of Jesus, by the hand of Jesus.

So it seems that we are left with two reasonably clear ends, and a most obscure middle. There is the tomb tradition: the apostolic band hears, on or around Easter Sunday, that the grave has been found empty on Sunday morning by one or more women rather loosely associated with Jesus' family or friends. And there is the mature conviction of the presence of Jesus in the community gathered for worship, a presence both judging and loving, an objective word from beyond, a summons and an invitation like the summons and invitation given in the days of his flesh. He is still personal, 'over against' his Church. And this conviction is focused upon the Lord's meal which is celebrated on the day of his resurrection. Between these two poles is Paul's list of names, a monumentally confusing jumble of incompatible stories, and little more. We can at least say that the initial experiences of conversion, recovery and restoration were understood as produced 'by Jesus' directly, not through the mediation of the community: that there *is* again a community depends upon an initiative from elsewhere, an initiative more positive than that provided simply by the report of the empty tomb. We can deduce what these experiences meant in terms of grace and hope, the restoring and forgiving of the past, the commission to preach; we can say nothing about what happened with any precision. As we have observed, the result is the creation of a new literature, stories which cannot be fitted into conventional moulds. The immediate response is in the formation of a community, and the record of individual encounter with the risen Jesus is instantly buried in the tradition-formations of the group—or rather of a large assortment of groups. That in itself tells us something significant about the 'apparitions': no one seems very interested in preserving a record of the visions of individuals. There are lists without details. And no one is disturbed at the thought of apparitions ceasing, no one develops a straightforward theology of Jesus' withdrawal. Luke comes closest to this: Jesus' Spirit acts as a surrogate for his presence in Acts. Yet there is no doubt that, in Acts, the apostolic commission and the power to do mighty works is inseparable from the *name* of Jesus, and it is in this name alone that forgiveness is granted. There is no effective denial of Jesus' abiding presence. Overall, we might say that the apparitions have no meaning independently of the establishment of the community; and if this is so, there is no reason for any interest in the detail of these encounters for its own sake.

The apparitions have no independent significance precisely because of what they in fact communicate. They are not simple manifestations of an apotheosized Jesus. If, as this essay has argued, they were fundamentally experiences of restoring grace, they take their places in a concrete, shared human history of hope, betrayal, violence and guilt, and are 'evidenced' *not* by individual report but by the continuing existence of the community in which this history is caught up and redeemed. To see the risen Jesus is to see one's own past and one's own vocation, to 'see' the call towards the new humanity. Of course the argument is circular: the 'apparitions' must have been like this because they are not remembered in any other context than the eucharistic, the gift-directed, life of the Church; the Church lives by Eucharist and gift because the resurrection encounters were experiences of the gift and the call of Jesus, restored to the world after his death. There is no hope of understanding resurrection outside the process of renewing humanity in forgiveness. We are all agreed that the empty tomb proves nothing; we need to add that no amount of apparitions, however well authenticated, would mean anything either apart from the testimony of forgiven lives communicating forgiveness. The life of Jesus, the truth that he is not exhausted and consumed by the world's mortal violence, is shown in the life of faith. 'While we live we are always given up to death for Jesus' sake, so that the life of Jesus may be manifested in our mortal flesh' (2 Cor. 4:11). The life of Jesus is shown in the community that meets to break bread with him, even when it has crucified him repeatedly, that gathers in repentant self-knowledge and in courageous hope.

It is frustrating, in a way, to end with such vagueness on

the substantive point of 'What Really Happened?'. But this is a deliberate choice. I may make a personal option in favour of a fairly 'objectivist' account of the resurrection, taking seriously the empty tomb as a sign of God's historical act of raising Jesus 'as a person' (as a 'body', in some sense): I find this extremely perplexing, and cannot give any very satisfactory theological or philosophical account of it, yet I find it the least difficult interpretation of the New Testament record. Other options are more easily defensible on other grounds, but all seem unduly to shrink the range and complexity of our narratives. However, I am not particularly concerned here with arguing the case for such an option. Part of the trouble with a good deal of modern debate on the resurrection is that it turns on the questions of 'What *happened* to Jesus?' or 'What *happened* to the apostles?' whereas the one thing we can say with confidence is that what happened to the world of men and women was the advent of the Church—of a new style of corporate human life—and of its proclamation of release from the prison of mutual destructiveness. The interesting theological question then becomes, 'How is this phenomenon, the advent of Church and gospel, grounded in the conviction of the return of Jesus of Nazareth from the dead in such a way that neither Church nor gospel would make sense without it?'

That is the question I have tried to engage with, to understand why the Christian gospel is the Easter gospel. It is not an investigation which can avoid the critical, literary and historical questions so amateurishly touched upon in this book, but equally it is not an investigation whose results depend wholly upon resolving certain of these questions in one way or the other. It is possible to be so preoccupied with the chronology of Easter Sunday and the subsequent weeks or months (or years), or with the endlessly intriguing literary history of the resurrection stories that the question of why the resurrection should be good news *now* almost disappears. And this can produce the reaction whereby 'resurrection' becomes simply a metaphor for grace, or triumph over adversity, or hope, or any other general human phenomenon, without its being related very clearly to the actual execution of a sup-

posed rebel and/or blasphemer by the Roman colonial admin-
istration. Between the Scylla of critical pedantry and the
Charybdis of vaguely religious psychology, this essay has
attempted to sail.

Its weakness, like the weakness of practically everything
written 'theologically' about Easter, stems, I think, from two
things. The first is this: we are often reminded these days of
the primacy in religious discourse of *story*. Certain things can
really only be dealt with in narrative terms, and are not
readily reducible to any kind of programmatic account. That
is why I have concentrated heavily on the resurrection stories
as stories, and also why I have referred from time to time to
other kinds of stories, such as modern fiction, in order to
make points not otherwise easily made. Nevertheless, this
book is not a narrative: it proposes some ways of reading or
hearing stories, and so risks imposing patterns and distorting
the simplicity of the narrative process. These risks are necessarily part of any interpretation or translation, of course, and
I make no apology: the 'weakness' is the overwhelming like-
lihood that a translation will paradoxically make a story more,
not less, alien for some because of the intrusion of the 'second
stranger', the translator.

The second reason is of a related kind. In this book, I have
argued that to speak of the resurrection of Jesus is also to
speak of one's own humanity as healed, renewed and restored,
re-centred in God; and the problems of talking about this are
thus the problems of describing where one stands and who
one is. You cannot see your own face, except in a mirror; you
cannot describe with satisfactory completeness and objectivity
the new life of grace except by looking at the resurrection of
Jesus. But 'the risen Jesus' only has clear content in relation
to the life of grace as experienced now (as we have seen, there
is no mileage in speculating about the Easter event in abstrac-
tion). Jesus' risenness and our risenness are visible only
obliquely, in relation to each other. And this means that they
are really uttered and manifested only in a speech that belongs
directly within that relationship, a speech that is an intrinsic
part of the process of discovering myself, and the human
future overall, in the presence of Jesus. This is a language of

worship and of active discipleship, a language that is 'eucharistic' in the extended sense given that word in this concluding chapter.

In this respect, of course, resurrection-language presents only the problems present in all Christian language, the problems of speaking about God and the human together, without confusion, without change, without division, without separation. In the preceding chapter, we saw how the risen Jesus presented in concrete and dramatic form the tension in Christian understanding between the familiar and the strange, and how a theoretical resolution of this on paper is not possible. 'Theologies' of Easter only do their job, perhaps, by their very theoretical untidiness, by their capacity to point back towards the disorienting 'He is not here' of the very first Easter witness; back to the confusing narratives and the frustrating impossibility of pinning down and defining 'the' Easter experience. If it can do this, an Easter theology, for all its failures, may (I hope) take its place within that process of the active and contemplative discovery of a new humanity to which the Easter gospel invites us. And John's Apocalypse provides something of a charter for the enterprise of theological witness:

> When I saw him, I fell at his feet as though dead. But he laid his right hand upon me, saying, 'Fear not, I am the first and the last, and the living one; I died and behold I am alive for evermore, and I have the keys of Death and Hades. Now write what you see. . . .'
>
> (Rev. 1:17–19)

Notes

1. Luke, by concluding his resurrection narratives with a visible 'lifting-up' of Jesus to heaven, simplifies the issues a little by postulating a period in which Jesus is 'risen', but not fully 'exalted'. He is rather more like a *revenant* here than elsewhere; but Luke is still emphatic about the unique nature of the risen flesh, which is not subject to ordinary material limitation. On the background of Rev. 1 in the

conventions of Jewish angelophanies, see the excellent study by C. C. Rowland, 'The Vision of the Risen Christ in Rev. i. 13ff: The Debt of an Early Christology to an Aspect of Jewish Angelology', in the *Journal of Theological Studies*, vol. XXXI pt. 1 (April 1980).

2. For examples of this, see Hennecke–Schneemelcher, *New Testament Apocrypha*, vol. I, section VII, especially pp. 253–9, 321–2, 341–4, 484–503.

3. Cf. Duquoc, *Christologie*, vol. II, *Le Messie* (Paris, Cerf, 1972), p. 253; cf. also p. 236.

4. And see the detailed study of Peter Selby, *Look for the Living. The Corporate Nature of Resurrection Faith* (SCM 1976), especially pp. 134–42.

5. Which is why the admittedly intriguing problems surrounding the Holy Shroud of Turin do not have any crucial theological import.

6. E.g., Schillebeeckx, *Jesus*, pp. 388–90; M. Goulder, in *The Myth of God Incarnate* (SCM 1977), p. 59; behind both stands W. Marxsen's classical and controversial account in *The Resurrection of Jesus of Nazareth* (SCM 1970), chap. 3.

7. See John O'Neill's most interesting paper, 'On the resurrection as an historical question', in *Christ, Faith and History*, edited by S. W. Sykes and J. P. Clayton, (CUP 1972), pp. 205–19, especially pp. 215–216.

8. See Marxsen's discussion, op. cit., chs. 4 and 5; and contrast Moore, *The Fire and the Rose Are One*, pp. 80–7.

9. Cf. Duquoc, op. cit., p. 237: 'The Resurrection does not abolish history in favour of an anticipated eternity, it establishes history in its most authentic dimension: openness to a future that is always new, the sole locus of responsibility before God'; and cf. p. 236: '[The Spirit] is sent to [the disciples] by the Risen One so that they may, in their own history, take on the mode of existence which was his own.'

10. Cf. Moore, *The Fire and the Rose are One*, pp. 80–1: 'For [the disciples], God had involved himself so much in the life and the movement of Jesus that the failure of the movement was much more like the death of God than his mere absence'; and 85 ('A Disciple Speaks'): 'This was as though all that we had believed about God were coming true'.

11. At the end of one traumatic and at times painfully polarized 'training weekend' on group process and interaction, the participants decided that they were not able to construct a eucharistic celebration together with any measure of integrity. This is a case in point (certainly involving a growth in truthfulness, and a rejection of 'cheap' reconciliation): whether we see it as a right or wrong decision, it is important to grasp why it might be a Christianly *possible* decision. On the social and political context of the Eucharist more generally, see Juan-Luis Segundo, s. J., *The Sacraments Today* (New York, Orbis Books, 1974), especially pp. 32–40, 59–62, 104–13.

12. See, e.g., Schillebeeckx, *Christ the Sacrament of the Encounter with God* (Sheed & Ward 1963), pp. 43–5.

13. On this concept, sometimes called, 'trans-signification', see Schillebeeckx, *The Eucharist* (Sheed & Ward 1968), pp. 148–50.
14. See Alexander Schmemann, *The World as Sacrament* (DLT 1966), especially the first and last chapters.
15. The phrase originates with Ignatius of Antioch, in his letter to the Ephesians (20.2).
16. *The Risen Christ and the Eucharistic World*, E.tr. René Hague (Collins 1976), p. 82.
17. Ibid., p. 195.
18. Ibid., pp. 83–4.
19. See Fuller, op. cit., pp. 109–10; and Oscar Cullmann, *Early Christian Worship* (SCM 1953), pp. 15–16.
20. This seems to be implied by Robert Leaney in his survey of 'Recent Studies on the Resurrection of Jesus', in *Theology and Change. Essays in Memory of Alan Richardson*, ed. Ronald H. Preston (SCM 1975), pp. 53–67, at p. 66.
21. For a very ancient account of the appearance to James, suggesting obliquely that it follows immediately on Jesus' leaving the sepulchre and abandoning his grave-clothes, see the fragment of the 'Gospel of the Hebrews' preserved by Jerome (*de vir. illus.* 2), Hennecke–Schneemelcher, op. cit., vol. I, p. 165. Note the strongly eucharistic cast of this narrative. It is at least as early as the first couple of decades of the second century.

Index

'Abba', 70–1, 84
acceptance of rejected, 108–9
Acts, 7–10, 19, 27, 50, 98, 117
adulthood, call to, 88
Ananias, 10
Anderson, R. S., 50
Annas, 9
anti-semitism, 18, 22, 28, 67
Apocalypse, 36, 121
apocalyptic delusion, 22–3
apostles, community of, 104, 115;
  see also Acts; disciples; James;
  John; Luke; Mark; Matthew;
  Paul; Peter; Thomas
apparition stories, 38–40, 44, 47,
  101–7, 116, 118, 123
ascension, 103, 121
Augustine, St., 31, 36–7, 87
Aulén, G., 28

baptism, 59–63, 68, 74
Barnes, M., 28
Barrett, C. K., 28, 74, 99
Barth, K., 4–6
Becker, E., 22, 28
Bell, G., 67
Bernanos, G., 24, 28
Bethge, E., 75
betrayal of Jesus, 2, 34–5, 40,
  45

body: of Christ, Church as, 84;
  risen, 100–23
Bonhoeffer, D., 67
Bowker, J., 98
bread: of life, 110: see also
  Eucharist; food
Brothers Karamazov, The (F. M.
  Dostoevsky), 13, 22, 28
Buddhism, 98
Bunyan, J., 57

Caiaphas, 9
Calvary, 77–87
Campion, E., 57
Cassian, St. J., 93
catholicity of Church, 64–5, 70, 75,
  90
change, possibility of, 81
Chardin, T. de, 113
child as victim, 13, 24
Chitescu, N., 64
Christ see Jesus
Church: catholicity of, 64–5, 70,
  75, 90; as community, 52–75
Clarke, B., 74
Cleopas, 82–3
community: of apostles, 104, 115;
  of resurrection, 52–75
compassion, 87, 98
condemnation, 26

125

confession, 37, 87
Confessions, 31, 36–7
conversion, 13, 16: of Paul, 10–11, 38–9, 51, 104; of Peter, 105–6; of Mary, 44–6
Conzelmann, H., 99
counter-violence, 18, 78
Courcelle, P., 51
crucifier, myself as, 80
crucifixion *see* Calvary
Cullman, O., 123

Daniel, 9
Davies, W. D., 28
death, 22–3, 60–1
denial by Peter, 2, 34–5, 40, 45
desertion *see* betrayal
desire, faith as purification of, 84–9, 98
disciples: betrayal by, 2, 34–5, 40, 45; concepts of Jesus, 14, 36; *see also* apostles
divinity, human arrogation of, 22; *see also* God
Dumitriu, P., 18–19
Duquoc, 102, 122

Easter: and baptism, 63; in Galilee, 17–51; in Jerusalem, 7–16
Eckhart, J., 93
ego *see* self
Eliot, T. S., 30, 32, 98
Epiphany, 74
Eucharist, 58–9, 68, 109–16, 122; *see also* food
evangelism *see* universalization
Evans, C., 40, 53
Evdokimov, P., 74
exclusivism, 12
excommunication, 56, 74
Exsultet, 33
Ezekiel, 54

'Fate', 15
faith, 103–4; as purification of desire, 84–9, 98
familiarity of stranger, 91–2

Farewell Discourses, 42, 103
Father, God as, 14, 70–3, 84, 92–4
fellowship, restoration of, 40
'fellow-sufferers', 77–81, 86
food, sharing of, 34, 39–40, 108–18; *see also* Eucharist
forgiveness, 52; impossibility of, 21
Four Quartets (T. S. Eliot) *see* Little Gidding
Fox, G., 57
freedom of risen Christ, 89–90
Friends, Society of, 74
Fuller, R. H., 99, 123
Fung, R., 51

Galilee, Easter in, 17–51
genocide, 17
God: as Father, 14, 70–3, 84, 92–4; grace of, 74, 107; and humanity, 95; Jesus as, 92–4; kingdom of, 63–4; memory of, 23; 'passive righteousness' of, 19; as 'presence', 29, 35; as Truth, 37; and victims, 15, 67, 78
Golding, W., 20
Görres, I., 28
Goulder, M., 122
grace: future, 42–3; of God, 74, 107; release of, 10
Great Assize, parable of, 87
Grollenberg, L., 28
guilt, 8, 51

Hague, R., 123
Halkes, C., 75
Harper, M., 74
Head of Creation, Jesus as, 36
healing, 9–10
heaven and earth, marriage of, 107
Hennecke, E., 99, 122–3
Herbert, G., 99
Herod, 8
Holocaust, 22, 67; *see also* anti-semitism
'home, being at', 90–1
hope, 19; and memory, 17–51
Hosea, 54, 105

hospitality of Jesus, 108–9; *see also* food
humanity: and God, 95; of Jesus, 25–6, 97, 111

identification with Calvary, 77–81
Ignatius of Antioch, 123
images, 72, 93
innocence, 13
inter-Church relations, 56
isolation of death, 60

James, St., 38, 117, 123
Jenkins, D., 80, 98
Jeremiah, 54
Jerome, 123
Jerusalem, Easter in, 1, 7–16
Jesus: apparitions of, 38–40, 44, 47, 101–7, 116, 118, 123; betrayal of, 2, 34–5, 40, 45; and death, 60–1, 77–87, 108–9; disciples' concepts of, 14, 36; as grace of God, 107; as God, 92–4; hospitality to marginal people, 108–9; humanity of, 25–6, 97, 111; as judge, 15; as king, 112–13; as law, 27–8; as love, 108; non-violence of, 13–14; and Peter, 35–6; as resource of meaning, 91; as salvation, 72; as Son of Man, 14; as symbol, 26; as truth, 41–2; as victim, 15, 19, 21; as Word, 36, 114
Job, 72
John, Gospel of: on apparitions, 39; on baptism, 61; on bread of life, 110; concepts of Jesus, 14, 36; on Farewell Discourses, 42; on Galilee, 35; on Mary Magdalene, 6, 44–7, 83, 88; and Peter, 39; on proof, 88, 103; on resurrection meals, 39; on Spirit, 52–3; on tomb, 106, 115
Joyce, J., 53
Judas, 24
judge, Jesus as, 15
judgement, 7–16, 53, 66

justification, 27

king, Jesus as, 112–13
kingdom of God, 63–4

Lampe, G. W. H., 16, 74
language, 69–73, 75, 86, 90, 121
'L'Arche' communities, 55
Last Supper, 39; *see also* Eucharist; food
Latimer, H., 57
law, Jesus as, 27–8
Le Blond, J.-M., 50
Leaney, R., 123
Lewis, S., 51
liberation: from self, 77; movements, 30–1
Little Gidding (T. S. Eliot), 30, 32, 98
Lohfink, G., 98
Lord of the Flies (William Golding), 20–1, 28
loss, sense of, 45
Lossky, V., 3, 74–5
love, 44, 51, 89, 108, 110
Luke, St.: on ascension, 103, 121; on baptism of death, 60; on body of Jesus, 100; on Cleopas, 82–3; on 'community of gift', 115; on Jerusalem, 1, 5, 7–11; on Last Supper, 39; on Peter, 97; on Spirit, 117; on tomb, 106
Luther, M., 19, 70, 77, 79

McCabe, H., 74
Mackey, J., 98
MacKinnon, D. M., 50
Marcuse, H., 31
marginal figures, 105–6, 108
Mark, St.: on baptism, 60; on Galilee, 33, 50; on hospitality, 108; on marginal figures, 106; on women, 86
Martelet, G., 113
martyrs, 56–8, 78–9, 82
Marxism, 64
Marxsen, W., 122

Mary Magdalene, 2, 6, 25, 44–7, 83, 88
Mary Tudor, 57
material world *see* body
Matthew, St.: on baptism, 59–60; concept of Jesus, 36; on Great Assize parable 87; and Galilee 33, 35, 50; on God the Father, 93–4; on judgement, 12; on tomb, 106
Maundy Thursday, 109–10
meals *see* food
meaning: resource of, 91; search for, 49
memory: God's, 23; and hope, 17–51; neutralization of, 20–1; as self, 31
Merton, T., 28
metanoia, 46
Metz, J. B., 3, 31, 50, 67, 75
ministry, 66
Moore, S., 3, 28, 51, 122
More, T., 57
Moule, C. F. D., 28
Muir, E., 96
Murdoch, I., 50, 77, 79, 85, 93, 98

Nagel, T., 50
name-giving, 70–2
narratives of resurrection, 33, 83, 96; *see also* apparition
neutralization of memory, 20–1
non-sacramental communities, 74
non-violence, 13–14, 62, 108

O'Collins, G., 50, 98
O'Mahony, P., 75
O'Neill, J., 122
Origen, 93
Orsy, L., 74
other, sufferer as, 87–9
otherness, 83

pain *see* violence
Palestinian Arabs, 17
'para-liturgies', 68
'passive righteousness', 19
past, recovery of, 30–48, 57

Paul, St.: on apparitions, 103, 107, 116–17; on baptism, 59–60; concept of Jesus, 36; on condemnation, 26; conversion of, 10–11, 38–9, 51, 104; on divided community, 110; and Galilee, 98; on grace of God, 74; as persecutor, 2, 58, 87; and Peter 38; as Saul, 10–11; on sins, 115; on Spirit, 43, 69–70
persecution, 2, 58, 87; *see also* victims
Peter, St.: 116–17, arrest of, 8, 10; as betrayer, 2, 34–5, 40, 45; conversion of, 105–6; fellowship with Jesus, 35–6; Luke on, 97; on non-violence, 13; and Paul, 38; and tomb, 99
Pilate, 8
possessiveness, 89
prayer, 92
'presence' of God, 29, 35
proof, 88, 103
prophecy, 54
protest, 54
'protology', 114
purification of desire, faith as, 84–9, 98

Qumran, 9

racialism, 16
Rahner, K., 74
Red and the Green, The (Iris Murdoch), 76–7, 79, 98
recognition, 34, 44, 46, 51
recovery of past, 30–48, 57
redemption, 9–10; from time *see* past
Reformation, 88
rejected, acceptance of, 108–9
renewal of humanity, 120
resurrection: and body, 100–23; community of, 52–75; in Galilee, 17–51; in Jerusalem, 7–16; and judgement, 7–16; and memory

and hope 17–51; and stranger, 76–99
Revelations, 98, 121
Ricoeur, P., 63
'righteousness, passive', 19
risen body, 100–23
Rowland, C. C., 122
Rupp, G., 28

salvation, Jesus as, 72
sanctification, 16
Saul see Paul
Schillebeeckx, E., 3, 51, 75, 98, 122–3
Schmemann, A., 123
Segundo, J.-L., 122
Selby, P., 122
self: decentring of, 85; -deception, 32, 65; -knowledge, 66; liberation from, 77; as memory, 31; myths of, 30; recovery of, 22, 36–48
sharing see Eucharist; food
Simon, U., 21
sin, 115; memory of 31; 'solidarity' in, 80
sinned-againstness, 51
Sinyavsky, A., 50
slavery, 65
Soelle, D., 75, 77–8, 98
Son of Man, 14
Southwell, R., 57
Speaight, R., 28
speech see language
Spirit, 52–3, 94, 117; gifts of, 43; and memory, 31; in Old Testament, 74; and speech, 69–71

Stein, D., 75
stories see apparitions
stranger, talking to, 34, 76–99
suffering: 'fellow-', 77–81, 86; and ourselves, 77–80; see also victims
suicide, 48
symbolism, 26, 68, 79

Teresa, Mother, 64
terrorism, 18, 78–9
testimony and manifestation, 63
Theology of Auschwitz (Ulrich Simon), 21
Thomas, St., 47, 88, 103
tomb, empty, 105–6, 115–16
transformation of world, 112
truth, 37, 41–3
turning back, 44, 46, 53

universalization, 11, 41, 47, 51
untruthfulness, 41–2

Vanier, J., 55, 74
victims, 10–27, 32, 78; memory of, 66–7
violence, 10–27; collusion in, 48, 77–87
vocation, 42–3: to catholicity, 64; and forgiveness, 35

war, 67
Weil, S., 15, 28
Wickremesinghe, L., 75
Williams, R., 75, 98
Wisdom, divine, Jesus as, 36
women, 65, 86, 106
Word, Jesus as, 36, 114

Zizioulas, J., 75